World Economics A

Book Series

Volume 8

A Philosophical Framework for Rethinking Theoretical Economics and Philosophy of Economics

Titles produced by the World Economics Association & College Publications

Volume 4
On the use and misuse of theories and models in mainstream economics
Lars Pålsson Syll

Volume 5
Green Capitalism. The God that Failed
Richard Smith

Volume 6
40 Critical Pointers for Students of Economics
Stuart Birks

Volume 7
The European Crisis
Victor Beker and Beniamino Moro, eds.

Volume 8
A Philosophical Framework for Rethinking Theoretical Economics and Philosophy of Economics
Gustavo Marqués

The **World Economics Association (WEA)** was launched on May 16, 2011. Already over 13,000 economists and related scholars have joined. This phenomenal success has come about because the WEA fills a huge gap in the international community of economists – the absence of a professional organization which is truly international and pluralist.

The World Economics Association seeks to increase the relevance, breadth and depth of economic thought. Its key qualities are worldwide membership and governance, and inclusiveness with respect to: (a) the variety of theoretical perspectives; (b) the range of human activities and issues which fall within the broad domain of economics; and (c) the study of the world's diverse economies.

The Association's activities centre on the development, promotion and diffusion of economic research and knowledge and on illuminating their social character.

The WEA publishes 20+ books a year, three open-access journals *(Economic Thought, World Economic Review* and *Real-World Economics Review)*, a bi-monthly newsletter, blogs, holds global online conferences, runs a textbook commentaries project and an eBook library.

www.worldeconomicassociation.org

A Philosophical Framework for Rethinking Theoretical Economics and Philosophy of Economics

Gustavo Marqués

ISBN 978-1-84890-223-7 print
ISBN 978-1-911156-33-8 eBook-PDF

Published by College Publications (London) on behalf of the World
Economics Association (Bristol)

http://www.worldeconomicsassociation.org
http://www.collegepublications.co.uk

Cover photo by Kyla Rushman
Cover design by Laraine Welch
Printed by Lightning Source, Milton Keynes, UK

Contents

Acknowledgement

I am deeply indebted to Edward Fullbrook who invested a lot of time in the revision of my book, alerting me about confusing paragraphs which had to be rewritten. He also gave me valuable suggestions for restating and improving many of my arguments.

Introduction

This book sets out to encourage a debate about the roles that economic theory and philosophy of economics can play. It starts by making a distinction between the domain of the economic processes and phenomena, and that of its representations. It is a crucial distinction that Sugden (2000) identified as the difference between the "real world" and the "model world". An insurmountable gap among them could exist. In fact, Sugden labels the model world as a "parallel" world, which triggers questions about whether a connection among them exists or not and how it should be characterized if it exists. Other authors have considered the possibility that economic models are autonomous from both theories and the facts of real market economies, which opens the door for claiming that they could be describing completely *imaginary* worlds. Is it possible that a good part of economics consists of theoretical developments that have no connections to actual market economies? The history of some branches of science shows that this possibility cannot be readily dismissed. Consider the history of anatomy during the XIV century in Europe. It was taught at universities, and the classes consisted of two different simultaneous activities. From his desk the teacher delivered a speech about the subject of the day. He was the academic authority in his classes. The content of the speech was taken from classical texts, some of them written during the III century before Christ (particularly by Galeno). Given the impossibility of dissecting cadavers (this practice was impeded by a legal disposition that prevailed during good part of the Middle Ages) the teacher had not had contact with the organs of real human bodies and literally repeated what Galeno wrote. The problem is that Galeno had not had access to human bodies either, and in some cases he attributed to humans what he observed in pigs and monkeys. Meanwhile at the center of the room a butcher and an auxiliary of the teacher were dissecting a cadaver to illustrate to the audience the main points of the lecture. But to their surprise what they saw was sometimes very different from what was taught. They were inhabitants of the *real* world but the teacher was living inside what may be called a *bookish world*.

In this book I argue that a good part of mainstream (and maybe some non-mainstream) economics may be in a situation that is similar to that of middle age anatomy: it is trapped inside the "model world", solving theoretical problems suggested by previous texts. The difference with the lessons of Anatomy described above is that what may be called *bookish theoretical economics* is relatively free form the authoritarian bias that dominated most of the Middle Ages, and that it has not only lessons to transmit but also puzzles to solve. But the fact persists that even if finding solutions to bookish oriented problems may be found exciting by the members of the community, they may be irrelevant for approaching the main economic problems of market economies. Traditionally epistemology also has suffered the bookish orientation bias too. Most epistemological texts refer less to the results of real scientific practice than to other epistemological texts. Epistemology has created so to say its own subject of research, approaching puzzles that are mainly interesting for philosophers not for practicing scientists. Mainstream philosophy of economics (MPE) is not the exception on this point.

Against this bias, in this book the priority of the ontological realm is assumed. One of its central tenets is that the "real" nature of the social world imposes restrictions on individuals' knowledge. The (objective) features of the intended target are central to deciding if it is possible or not to use theories and models to obtain scientific (that is to say, relevant and reliable) knowledge of it and what type of technologies can be implemented on this basis. If the purpose of theoretical and philosophical analysis in economics is to make a contribution to find out how modern market economies work and which kind of theoretical practice will be useful for the implementation of successful economic policies, a shift both in philosophy of economics and economics itself is needed in order to comply with those restrictions that the nature of the phenomena imposes on them. The prevailing bookish orientation must be replaced for an analysis of economic processes.

Introduction

Going beyond bookish orientation in economics

Theoretical models built within the bookish orientation offer arbitrary and imaginary models designed to solve theoretical problems posed by antecedent models. One of the main assumptions of this book is that a correct characterization of the main traits of the subject under examination has preeminence over the set of strategies designed to understand it. If theoretical practice in economics is going to have authentic epistemic relevance, it is necessary to shift the attention from standard models developed within the current bookish tradition to the solution of those concrete problems which result from open ended, intervenible and conflictive economic processes, dominated by radical uncertainty. I characterize them in some detail in Chapter Five.

A processes oriented economics would have to provide a different kind of theoretical practice adequate for examining *sequences of feasible economic events* (i.e., the main developments that those processes could plausibly adopt). This kind of practice offers points of intervention to those skills, qualifications, common sense and political abilities that are needed to manage these processes. The accomplishment of one of the several plausible sequences will be the product of a combination of all these practical capabilities that belong to what may be called "management and lobbyist practice". The subjects of this practice are both the action of the state (which wrongly has been traditionally identified as the only interventionist actor) and the lobby of the many diverse groups able to influence the economy. Their joint actions determine the state of the economic phenomena at each stage of the process.

In order to avoid misunderstandings it is worth clarifying from the beginning that even those most arbitrary and imaginary conventional models do not have anything wrong *per se*. They can be conceived as "intellectual exercises" designed to solve theoretical problems and nothing erroneous can be found in such a practice. This book has not been written against standard economic theory. What I maintain, rather, is that theoretical practice in economics can be something *different from the strategy* that places theoretical models at the center of the scene. In this sense, this book contains a call for reorienting economic theory which is consistent with a

3

pluralistic view: it states that there is *another object* - the concrete economic processes- that demands attention. The emergence of a Non-bookish Economics is possible and desirable, one which could perfectly coexist with imaginary model-building practice and that focuses on how *real* markets work.

Going beyond mainstream philosophy of economics

But the central purpose of this book is to make an exhortation for reorienting the current philosophy of economics. To start, it has failed to solve the purpose that it imposes on itself, to show the superiority of "scientific" over "verbalistic" economics, and to support the epistemic relevance of bookish oriented models. In fact, *mainstream philosophy of economics* (MPE) has misunderstood the nature of the kind of economic practice which it intends to "recover". MPE is mistaken about what the aims of conventional modeling practice are. Although philosophy of economics is perfectly entitled to limit its analysis to conventional economic representations (and their results can be illuminating in this dominion), there are solid reasons to claim that mainstream modeling does not try to represent our world, but just to solve theoretical problems. If it wishes to recover this practice, the kind of problems that theoretical mainstream models attempt to solve should be correctly identified. I claim that conventional economics is better understood as "intellectual exercises".

More importantly, MPE has failed to show the supposed superiority of "scientific" (as opposed to "verbalistic") economics. MPE claims that theoretical standard models do contain reliable knowledge about our world, but it admits that more and better additional knowledge is needed to show that these models' are up to this task. However, as long as such knowledge external to the models belongs to "background knowledge" (composed by common sense, disciplinary wisdom, "trained smell", etc.), MPE reintroduces the many types of skills and knowledge that two hundred years ago economic theory, driven by its pretension to being scientific, tried to overcome. Philosophers of bookish economics seem to be in the same weak position of the "Teachers" of Anatomy who were overcome for the rough practice of the butcher!

4

But my main objection is that MPE has ignored or dismissed the many theoretical and philosophical problems arising from open-ended processes. It insists in treating them as lawfully or mechanistically commanded processes and strives to validate the epistemic relevance of bookish oriented models. Going beyond MPE means to incorporate into the agenda an analysis of the ontological features of economic processes, to call attention to the decisive role of the practice of lobbing, and to address such problems as rationality, learning and useful theoretical practice under uncertainty. The present book offers an outline of how this task could be performed.

Science and economics

Let me advance a brief comment about the relation between science and economics. This book does not take an irrational or anti-scientific stance. On the contrary, in the domain of natural phenomena modern science has shown extraordinarily successful results. But the same cannot be said when social processes are at stake, and I have tried to offer some of the reasons (ultimately, ontological) for this failure. So, I do not share the idea of those authors who think that economics can be scientific (as much as natural sciences), and that such an economic theory, once found, would solve those economic problems that the best theoretical tradition assigned to economics a long time ago (growth, employment and development with fairness and equality).

Particularly, I think that the dream of having a successful theory of expectation formation is largely a chimera, and indeed I dismiss the necessity of having such a theory. Neither governmental authorities nor any other economic actor may count on being able in a sure (scientific) way to intervene and make people entertain "correct" expectations. But as we try to show in this book economic actors (including the state) do not need a scientific theory able to guarantee their goals in order to intervene systematically upon the economy. Instead they can apply feasible sequences as well as direct (practical) knowledge and skills to cope with the situation and push the process in the desired direction.

5

It is also important to examine the relation between science and economics from another perspective. Theoretical physics has been successfully applied to a wide range of circumstances of our world. This could be done thanks to the development of associated technologies (different kinds of engineering, founded on physical theory). Some may think that nowadays economics is at a pre-technological stage (like physics was sometime ago), and that what is needed is more time (and more knowledge, mainly mathematical knowledge) to develop a sort of economic engineering. Popper was confident in the benefits of fragmentary social engineering. The call to elaborate an alternative economics oriented to solve practical problems of our world could be interpreted this way.

Our analysis of deliberate mechanisms like Prospect Theory and Decision Making Models gives testimony of the kind of practical results that can be obtained by this road. But I suspect that in reference to more traditional economic problems like those mentioned at the beginning of this section, a similar expectation is unfounded and doomed to failure. As far as economic phenomena result from open ended processes as we have described them there is no possibility of shaping and controlling them by means of social engineering similar to what happens in the case of natural sciences. The social technologies that we analyze in Chapter Four are limited to very specific domains where neither uncertainty nor conflicts between lobbyists that defend different and opposite interests exist. These technologies are not designed for "leading" in a scientific way the economic processes. And I suspect that it is not possible to hope that we may count on similar tools in the near future.

A constructivist vision of social processes

The Hayekean and Popperian programs for social sciences considered that their main task was to find out those not deliberately pursued (and often not wished) consequences of our actual decisions. This program presupposes that laws or mechanisms acting on the back of individuals' consciousness commanded economic phenomena in an independent and inexorable way. This is the main program of Bookish Economics and to back such approach is the main task of mainstream philosophy of economics. To this program I oppose a different one in which, given open-ended and intervenible

6

economic processes based on expectations, lobbyers strive to attain (often successfully) consequences they desire. In fact, this is the whole point for the existence of lobbying!

Our approach emphasizes the *deliberate* aspect of the interventionist behavior and the possibility that such strategy may be successful. It perceives social and economic sequences less as commanded by spontaneous or designed mechanisms and more as open ended and intervenible processes constructed by the joint actions of the many mutually conflicting agents. It is more enlightening to think of them as systems similar to the Lego game, as described in Chapter Five, and not as a vending machine.[1] Non bookish economics is much more like politics than science.

The present book is a pluralist text, both with regard to economic theory and to philosophy of economics. No attempt to impede scholars from doing bookish economics or mainstream philosophy of economics is here advanced. Instead I claim that another object of analysis for both disciplines exists (real economies and the nature of the processes that form them), and that they are relevant, attractive and require urgent treatment.

The general plan of the book is as follows.

Part I offers a criticism of MPE (of its goals and its success in recovering the practice of mainstream economic theory). The actual mainstream philosophy of economics takes the *model* as its unit of epistemic analysis. This view does not approach real economies but instead their representations. It is then a philosophy of conventional economic representations, and one of its main purposes is "to recover" conventional theoretical practice. "Recovering" means to analyze conventional models (to describe their components, to see

---

[1] "Nature is rife with what I call nomological machines, from clocks and vending machines to seeds and caterpillars. The machines of interest here involve a relatively stable arrangement of parts which gives rise to a number of interconnected causal processes inside the machine plus some kind of skin or shield that limits access to the internal variables under a variety of common circumstances. We put the coins in and get out a packet of crisps; we do not perform key-hole surgery on the vending machine to jiggle the levers and chutes inside" (Cartwright, 2007a, p. 18).

how their theoretical resources are employed, what types of idealizations are used, etc.) and, overall, to *justify* them: to show that they do offer relevant and reliable knowledge about this object of study (presumably, some aspect of real economies). MPE's attitude comes from its commitment to naturalism, a philosophical view that grants that science provides the best available knowledge, and its belief that standard bookish theoretical economic practice *is* scientific.

Two main approaches exist regarding the construction, nature and function of theoretical models, and I will designate them as *isolationist* and *autonomist*. In this book I mainly examine the first of these approaches: the isolationist vision. A central problem that the isolationist perspective must solve is to show how theoretical models are related to their "intended targets". And these connections must be argued taking into consideration two important restrictions: a) to avoid the traditional criticisms of mainstream models because of their "unrealism"; b) to dismiss the fact that economic models usually lack successful relevant applications. Under these conditions, how can the relevance and trustworthiness of the knowledge provided by them be defended? It will be argued that MPE has managed to defend mainstream models from the accusations of unrealism. But I intend to demonstrate that MPE does not offer good arguments for excusing mainstream models for their scant record of successful empirical applications. Given this failure I maintain that theoretical modeling in economics is better understood if conceived as mere intellectual exercises, without representative or applied vocation. The third chapter supports the claim that the economy does not need models to refer to economic processes and phenomena, showing that economics is intricately linked with the rest of the disciplines that study other domains of the social field.

Part II of the book examines some successful uses of the mechanistic conception within economics and questions the extent to which this approach may contribute to successful economic technologies. Two interesting cases of technological application of some branches of the economic theory are examined: Libertarian Paternalism (LP)–based on Prospect Theory (PT) – and Mechanisms Design (MD). The special conditions that explain their successful application, as well as the limitations that this strategy outside the narrow domain in which it has been tried are analyzed. It is argued that Mechanism Design's dominion of application is very limited and neither concerns nor contributes to the solution of most traditional economic problems, those that most people would like economics to help solve. Even worse, in one of the cases where these technologies are more successful (the so-called Libertarian Paternalism), the foundation comes from a heterodox theory of decision making (Prospect Theory), which deeply dislikes the orthodoxy of MPE.

Chapter Five begins the analysis of one of the main topics of the book: the special features of economic processes based on agents' expectations, which are dominated by uncertainty in the radical (Keynesian) sense of the term. Its open-ended nature is considered as well as the role that the intervention (lobby) of a variety of economic actors with conflicting interests plays in them. It is argued that under these conditions both the conventional modeling strategy and the mechanistic perspective lack sustentation. Particularly, the analysis reveals that insurmountable difficulties exist for extending technologies of the Mechanism Design or Libertarian Paternalism type to the domain of economic processes.

Part III of the book extracts some philosophical consequences from the previous analysis and offers an outline of the way in which the practice in theoretical economics and philosophy of economics could be reoriented. Chapters Six and Seven focus on some of the difficulties that arise in order to give sense to key economic concepts - like rationality, learning and testing - when uncertainty is assumed. Particular attention is paid to the rationality assumption and some of the main arguments that have been offered to defend its legitimacy under conditions of uncertainty. In Chapter Eight the main ideas of the book are synthesized and two fundamental shifts in approaching economics and philosophy of economics are advocated: (1) the promotion of a new kind of theoretical approach to economics that takes into account uncertainty, conflict of interests and the systematic intervention of a great variety of lobbyists; (2) the generation of a different way of doing philosophy of economics that (a) elucidates and clarifies the particular features of economic processes and (b) clarifies the type of theoretical knowledge that can be acquired by those processes, as well as the type of knowledge and skills which are at disposal of economic actors (agents and lobbyists).

The shift proposed means that a *scientific* approach like the one assumed by the usual way of modeling can be of little use either for analyzing market operations or as a guide for implementing efficient policies. The nature of economic processes suggests that it would be far more useful to apply a *political* analysis able to reveal their open-ended nature and the diversity of economic interests at play than a supposedly scientific analysis which aspires to find invariant laws, mechanisms or regularities.

Part 1

The nature and function of theoretical economic models – problems of mainstream philosophy of economics

Introduction

Traditional philosophy of science assumes that theories are the privileged unit of analysis of scientific knowledge, and that all reference to our world is made by them. Models are put in a second place and conceived as constructions made from theories and examined only in relation with them. Two main views about models have predominated. The syntactic vision of theories offers a clear way to differentiate theories from models, indicating that theories are systems of non-interpreted statements and models are those interpretations of their descriptive terms that make them true[1]. The subsequent semantic conception of models has blurred this distinction, claiming that theories *are* their models. Both of them, nevertheless, have argued that the concepts of model and theory are intimately related. Nowadays most of the authors who are interested in the subject refer to theories and models as different things, with the result that the entailment among them is considered much more tenuous than in the past. Endowing models with autonomy and relative independence with regard to theories has allowed seeing them as objects of privileged philosophical interest, placing them at the center of the scene.

> "For most of the 20th century, the use of models in science was a neglected topic in philosophy. Far more attention was given to the nature of scientific theories and laws. Except for

---

[1] It is the sentential view of theories, which was shared by logical empiricism and the Popperian philosophy of science.

a few philosophers in the 1960's, Mary Hesse in particular, most did not think the topic was particularly important. The philosophically interesting parts of science were thought to lie elsewhere. As a result, few articles on models were published in the twenty-five years following Hesse's (1966). The situation is now quite different. As philosophers of science have come to pay greater attention to actual scientific practice, the use of models has become an important area of philosophical analysis" (Koperski, 2006, IEP, p.1)

Models are however very fuzzy objects. Some decades ago this label was applied to some theoretical constructions that were somehow sub-products of theories[2]. Now things have changed. As Koperski points out "the word 'model' is highly ambiguous, and there is no uniform terminology used by either scientists or philosophers" (IEP, 2006). Firstly, a clear way for distinguishing between theories and models is not at hand[3]. This is particularly true in economics where both concepts are used practically as synonyms. On the other hand, given that the term "theory" is used with few restrictions, the domain of application of the word model has been expanding almost without limits. Knuuttila (2004, pp. 1 - 2) for instance argues that "the things called models in science are truly heterogeneous ensembles. They can be diagrams, physical three-dimensional things, mathematical equations, computer programs, organisms and even laboratory populations". Mäki (2005) considers that experiments also deserve to be taken as models.

In this chapter we examine the nature and function of a particular type of economic model: the *theoretical* models, which have been described by some authors as caricatures (Gibbard and Varian, 1978) or, more to the

---

[2] As Bunge (1982, chap. 4) said, models have a narrower domain than theories. So, for instance, we may talk of a theory of a whole economy, but a model of a factory of shoes.

[3] "...we do not see ourselves as providing a 'theory' of models. The latter would provide well-defined criteria for identifying something as a model and differentiating models from theories" (Morgan and Morrison, 1999, p.12). The "we" probably refers to both co-authors but it is valid on a wider domain. In fact there is no adequate and precise distinction between both concepts within the specialized literature.

point, as analogous economies (Lucas 1981a, pp. 7-8). We examine some of the main reasons that MPE has used to defend the relevance and trustworthiness of their cognitive role. This will allow us to evaluate its claim that theoretical models provide a special type of knowledge whose obtention would be difficult or impossible without them, and the even stronger claim that models are useful (and even necessary) to understand the workings of market economies and to design and implement economic policies.

There are two main conceptions about the nature of theoretical models that specify what kind of entities they are and what their function is: models as *isolations*, and models as *independent constructions*. Currently both visions concentrate the attention of Mainstream Philosophy of Economics and both of them generate interesting epistemic and philosophical problems. In this chapter we will examine the first conception. The autonomist vision will be addressed in the following chapters.[4]

For many philosophers the isolation procedure is the central tool of theoretical economic models. We will clarify this method and examine to what extent the claim that it contributes to discovering relevant and reliable causal knowledge in economics can be supported. Some of the main reasons that have been advanced in their favor, as well as some of the arguments that question their usefulness will be evaluated.

---

[4] Another perspective which has recently received attention is the normative concept of economic models (Hands, 2009). In order to keep the text within a reasonable length we are not going to address this issue here.

Rethinking theoretical economics and philosophy of economics

Chapter 1
The isolationist view

Those who think that the real world (target) is too complex to be analyzed *in toto*, are prone to believe that a wise strategy for acquiring knowledge about it is to shift the attention from the world itself to a more easily treatable object that somehow represents it. Models are often used in this substitutive role. When that happens, Mäki calls them *subrogate* models. Typically models involve diverse conceptual strategies that distort or omit some aspects of the target that the model sets out to investigate. However, in the past, conventional economic models have been criticized for employing "unrealistic" suppositions and disapproved for this very reason. The debate about the usefulness of adopting unrealistic assumptions is still ongoing.

In what may be considered an important contribution to the classic debate about the realism of economic assumptions, Musgrave (1981) showed that many of the statements supporting the presentation of economic models, which were considered false when taken in a literal sense, mean something quite different from what they were usually supposed to mean. He claimed that when properly interpreted, these assumptions may well be true. A similar approach is advocated in Lipsey & Steiner, 1981.[1] More recently Mäki (2008) made additional important remarks helping to understand the role of stylizations (idealizations, distortions and omissions) in the construction of economic models, claiming that their occurrence within a model is not an indicator of bad theoretical practice. These contributions have managed to undermine the realistic attack on conventional economic

---

[1] "Consider a theory that assumes the government has a balanced budget. This may mean that the theorist intends that theory to apply only when there is a balanced budget; it may *not* mean that the size of the government's budget surplus or deficit is irrelevant to the theory" (Lipsey and Steiner, 1981, p. 24).

models, showing that its arguments are not enough to reject mainstream models as carriers of true information about the world.

Mäki's rejection of traditional criticisms of economics goes even further and asserts that it is *possible* that economic models, even those that isolate ideal mechanisms or include any alleged "unrealistic" feature, *can* nonetheless *be true*.

> "Many of my arguments are 'even-if' arguments: Even if this and that, this model or explanation may be true. Even if its assumptions are false, a model may be true. Even if the model dramatically simplifies real-world phenomenon immensely complex, it may be true (......). This I take as sufficient for realism about truth in economics" (Mäki, 2008).

To the extent that his arguments are successful, they show that the reasons usually directed against traditional economic models are not good reasons for that purpose. They are just *negative* arguments, designed to criticize the critic's criticisms. Although they are able to defeat those traditional objections, they do not manage to dissipate the reluctance that many practicing economists feel with respect to the performance of idealized economic models. For example consider Mäki's initial comments of his 2002 Reading about the status of Economics:

> "Fact or fiction? Is economics a respectable and useful reality-oriented discipline or just an intellectual game that economists play in their sandbox filled with imaginary toy models? Opinions diverge radically on this issue, which is quite embarrassing from both the scientific and the political point of view (...) Economics is a contested scientific discipline. Not only are its various theories and models and methods contested but, remarkably, what is contested is its status as a science. (...) Suppose we take one of the characteristics of science to be the capability of delivering relevant and reliable information about the world. Suppose furthermore that this is not just a capability, but also a major goal and actual achievement of whatever deserves to be

called by the name of 'science'. How does economics do in this respect? This question is about as old as economics itself" (Mäki, 2002, p. 3).

It sounds really odd because these doubts do not arise (at least, not with this intensity) in the case of other sciences. Who may seriously doubt that physics or biology are "able to provide relevant and reliable information about the world"? It seems that there is a particular difficulty to understand the theoretical practice in economics, whose usefulness has not been clarified yet in spite of the fact that this issue has been debated for more than two centuries. To set aside the usual critics about the alleged *unrealism* of mainstream economic models offering negative reasons may be enough. Nevertheless, to help economists to feel proud of their models and philosophers of economics be in a better position to justify their explanatory capability and their practical value for the implementation of economic policies, additional reasons, this time *positive*, must be offered. Next we will examine some of the modeling procedures that have been rejected as unrealistic, with special emphasis on two of them: isolation and the addition of tractability suppositions, assessing some of the main arguments that have been offered in their favor. Before examining these questions it is convenient to introduce some lexical precisions.

We will designate as "stylizations" or "stylized" suppositions any type of alteration that representations (models) show with respect to their intended targets. There are three main classes of stylizations: (a) distortions: factors that are present in the target and are incorporated to the model in a distorted form; (b) omissions: those factors present in the target but omitted within the model, and (c) additions: factors nonexistent in the intended target but included within models for reasons of analytical convenience. These three types of stylizations generate three varieties of "unrealism", which we will designate, respectively, as unrealism by distortion, omission and addition. Although theoretical models can incorporate all sorts of stylizations, the traditional discussion around the realism of the assumptions has insisted on the two first forms. According to this view distortions are characteristics of caricatures, and omissions are at the center of the procedure of Isolation. Only recently has it been noted that theoretical economic models usually incorporate a particular class of stylization: the addition of a bunch of tractability suppositions.

Isolation

According to the isolation view, models are constructed incorporating some features of their intended targets and setting aside many other traits which are not considered relevant for the purposes intended in modeling. As Mäki says

> "In an *isolation*, something, a set X of entities, is 'sealed off' from the involvement or influence of everything else, a set of Y entities; together X and Y comprise the universe" (Mäki, 1992, p. 321).

This procedure generates his distinction between "isolated" and "excluded" fields[2]. Although Mill did not use this terminology, "isolation" is present in his idea that economics is an incomplete science because it has identified (and incorporated) "the mayor" causes of the economic phenomena, but not those "smaller" ones which remain out of theoretical consideration. This kind of knowledge provides *tendency* laws: laws that describe not the observable behavior of a phenomenon but a tendency to behave in such way. Nonetheless to count with knowledge of the *main* causes makes it possible to render account of the *major* part of that behavior. It seems to be a remarkable achievement for economics after all!

However the value of having such knowledge has been contested since the early times of Ricardo's *Principles*. In fact, many (perhaps most) economists of his time felt some sense of discomfort and even perplexity regarding their theories and models, the very same sensations experienced later by Mäki himself as a young student of economics (see Mäki, 2009). Thus in his Prefatory Notice (1859), William Whewell disputes the practical utility of a

---

[2] The concept of "unrealism" is somewhat vague and much more general than the concept of isolation, because usually it also refers to intellectual operations such as distortions and additions. The procedure of isolation instead is based on the conceptual operation of omissions.

theory that focuses exclusively on the workings of the main economic tendencies. He maintains that although such tendencies were in existence everywhere and in any time, their contribution to the explanation of key economic phenomena, like the distribution of income in the countryside, would be insignificant.

> "This doctrine of a universal tendency in the social world to reduce rents to the form of the Ricardian definition, we may perhaps be allowed to illustrate by saying that it is, as if a mathematical speculator concerning the physical world should teach, as an important proposition, that all things tend to assume a form determinated by the force of gravity: that thus, the hills tend to become plains, the waterfalls to eat away their beds and disappear, the rivers to form lakes in the vallies, the glaciers to pour down in cataracts. To which the reply would be, that the tendencies are counteracted by opposite tendencies of the same order, and thus have only a small share in shaping the earth's surface. The cohesion of rocks, the tenacity of ice, the original structure of mountains, are facts as real as the action of gravity; and the doctrine that the earth's surface tends to a level, is of small value and limited use in physical geography. And just so the original structure of nations, their early history, customs, and habits determine the tenure of land, and the relation of a cultivator to the classes above him, in a degree indefinitely greater than the mobility of capital and the consequent changes of tenure" (Whewell, 1859, p. xvi).

He agrees with the perspective of another contemporary author who asserts that,

> "(T)he real difficulty does not, therefore, lie in discussing matters connected with this science, in the statement of general principles, or in reasoning fairly from them; but it lies in the discovery of the secondary or modifying principles, which are always in action, and in making proper allowance

for their influence. Food is indispensable to existence; and it may, therefore, be laid down as a general principle, that this necessity on the one hand, and the difficulty of getting food on the other, tend to make every man die of hunger. Such, however, and so powerful are the countervailing influences, that not one individual out of 10.000 dies of want; and such being the case, a theory which should overlook these influences would not, we think, be good for much" (McCulloch, 1849, p. xiv).

Both authors doubt the value of Ricardo and Mill's strategy for providing relevant knowledge of real market economies. They argue that economics cannot leave out of consideration how "the smaller" causes affect the economic events. To my understanding, an even stronger interpretation of both arguments could be offered, which asserts that in itself the distinction between "major" and "minor" causes makes no sense, provided that in any particular case a certain disposition of "smaller" factors could completely inhibit the role of "the greater" ones.

Nancy Cartwright has undertaken a staunch defense of the method of isolation that at first sight seems to avoid the difficulties pointed out by Whewell and McCulloch. A central piece of her argument is a distinction between two types of results: "facts about what happens in the real economy" and "facts about stable tendencies". She claims that the purpose of theoretical economic models is not "*to establish results in our analogue economies that will hold outside them when literally interpreted. Frequently what we are doing in this kind of economic theory is not trying to establish facts about what happens in the real economy but rather, following John Stuart Mill, facts about* stable tendencies" (Cartwright, 1999, her italics).

A tendency is identified "isolating" the influence of a single cause (or set of causes) and showing what its "pure" (or "natural") contribution to the generation of those facts "that happen" in real economies is.

"What counts as 'isolation'? At the most general level the best we can say is that a cause is isolated (for purposes of ascertaining its causal power) when everything that can interfere with the production of the natural effect of the related causal power is absent (or, more realistically, calculated away) and all the helping and triggering factors necessary for the natural effect associated with the power to be produced are present" (Cartwright, 2007a (CP)).

Note that Cartwright emphasizes *not* the fact that isolation captures the *main* causes of a phenomenon, but the fact that the tendencies already known are *stable*, and she claims that what is known about a factor is its *pure* or *natural* causal power. This conceptual displacement has important consequences. At first sight Cartwright's argument has a Solomonic flavor: it recognizes the grain of truth "really" contained in the objections of McCulloch and Whewell, but eludes its catastrophic effect for economic theory. Although the objectors are right in that knowledge obtained by means of isolation does not serve to account for a phenomenon in its integrity (that which indeed happens), isolating *any* cause (major or small) is still relevant because it provides *universally valid knowledge about its pure contribution to a given effect.*

Criticisms of the isolationist view

The improved version of the method of "isolation" in economics replaces the problem of ascertaining the cause of a given effect for the problem of ascertaining the particular contribution of a factor to generate this effect. Anyway it has received several criticisms that focus on (a) the unavoidable presence of suppositions that are included only for tractability reasons, (b) the apparently insurmountable difficulty to add the diverse causal factors which have been separately isolated, and (c) the fact that social phenomena constitute totalities whose components are internally related, which means that social totalities cannot be analyzed by means of isolation without destroying them. Let's take a look at the most significant criticisms.

1. Overconstraint

In Cartwright's view both economics and physics "use the analytic method: they ascertain the behaviour that would result from the operation of a cause 'in isolation'; then take this behaviour to provide the 'contribution' that that cause makes to the behaviour that occurs *even when the cause is not in isolation*" (Cartwright, 2007a; my italics). An implication of this view is that A's capacity to contribute to B *is not* contextually dependent, but the ability of A to in fact generate B is. This is a remarkable result for those who advocate isolation: it means that it is a method that provides *universally valid* results. If this pretension were true it would be clear in what sense it can be said that theoretical models afford "relevant and reliable" knowledge.

However, not all that glitters is gold. The "pure" capacity of a given factor is only identified if it operates in an empty context. Otherwise the exhibited capacity is a function of the joint influence of that factor *and* those other factors that constitute the environment. In that case it is more appropriate to talk of the capacity that this factor shows *within a context such as that*. Acting in a different context the same factor can exhibit a completely different capacity. Cartwright admits this:

> "Models' results, I have argued, are frequently over-constrained by structural assumptions, and often necessarily so. I have raised this as an objection to the view that models can act as (...) thought experiments to investigate the 'natural' manifestations of capacities, that is, the manifestations that result purely from the exercise of that capacity alone" (Cartwright, 2007a).

In a later contribution she reinforces this position: even in the paradigmatic case of a single body moving within an empty universe over-determination still exists because some type of geometry has to be assumed (Cartwright, 2010).

The incorporation of this kind of additional suppositions (which Cartwright sometimes designates as "non-Galilean" or "structure") is a procedure that is not intrinsic to isolation (as it was defined), but something that this method cannot avoid. If the phenomenon of overconstraint cannot be eliminated, it means that it can never be said that a factor is considered in conditions of complete isolation. So, her claim that tendency models are able to provide some kind of *universally valid knowledge for our world, relevant and reliable*, collapses.

2. Social systems are not mechanical systems

But suppose that the problem of overconstraint could be avoided and a way by which models of tendencies were able to recognize the pure contribution of a set of causes to its effect were found out. The value of this achievement would be considerably diminished if on a second step the individual contributions could not be added. The aggregation of all these tendencies would be possible provided some procedure for their composition was available and the result of their joint actions could be showed. When these conditions apply it is said that the phenomenon is *mechanical*. The parallelogram of forces is the most representative example of a mechanical phenomenon.

It is doubtful however that the mechanical analogy can be illuminating for economics, because any law of composition requires that all the forces at play should be of the same type. Cartwright has pointed out that this is hard to find within the domain of social events, where the many influencing factors may be qualitatively different.

> "The trouble for economics with the mechanics analogy is that it supposes that everything that affects the manifest result in question is a cause of the same kind: each is an independent cause that has its own tendency law whose result will get treated in the law of composition. This seems to work in mechanics, where we make the assumption that everything besides initial position and velocity that affects a motion is a force and all the forces have their own tendency laws and all their consequences are handled by the law of composition. In this case the notion of a Galilean experiment makes perfect sense: in the experiment the force under study is to be introduced and all other forces are to be eliminated. This idea falls apart in typical economics cases. Preferences to live in neighborhoods of given colour mixes can have fixed capacities. Trivially these preferences are exercised when they are acted on. But the manifest results do not depend only on other causes with their own tendency laws dictating their own consequences that can be treated in

a law of composition, and this is so no matter how sophisticated we get about laws of composition. In reality the manifest results depend on structural circumstances and not just on the exercise of other capacities, even in principle. So it is not a surprise that the same should be true in the model" (Cartwright, 2007a, p. 75).

Other authors (like Hausman, 1992, and Hands, 2010) have also emphasized this point. This means that even supposing that "isolation" were able to show a particular (pure) contribution of each cause to the generation of a phenomenon (something that we have seen is not the case), a way to use that knowledge is not at hand because a general procedure to integrate the different isolated results is lacking. What purpose is served by isolation then?

3. Organic wholes

Introducing a distinction between abstracting and isolating, Tony Lawson has offered a different criticism of the method of isolation.

> "I interpret abstraction, here as always, according to its traditional meaning of focusing upon certain aspects of something to the (momentary) neglect of others. It is a process of focusing on some feature(s) of something(s) while others remain in the background. For example, in considering the ability of copper to conduct electricity well I may focus upon its atomic structure and thereby abstract from its colour, texture, malleability and so on" (see Fullbrook, 2008, p. 203)

Here abstraction means omission. This practice is unavoidable in the scientific activity and there is nothing wrong with it. But, according to Lawson, there is a difference between the intellectual operation of omitting (abstracting) and what Mäki denominates "isolation". Let us remember that in Mäki's view,

The isolationist view

"In an *isolation*, something, a set X of entities, is 'sealed off' from the involvement or influence of everything else, a set of Y entities; together X and Y comprise the universe" (Mäki, 1992, p. 321).

Lawson offers what seem to be four different arguments against isolation. First, he maintains that in the case of factors causally related, isolation (unlike abstraction) introduces falsehood in the model and lacks the capacity to contribute to an understanding of the economic causal relations. The falsehood to which he refers does not come from the fact that the isolating model incurs omissions or distortions (even idealizations). The problem with isolation is that it denies the existing connection between the factors incorporated to the model and the omitted ones. Being factors X and Y causally connected within target T, to isolate X amounts to (a) to jointly affirm X and the non-existence of Y, or (b) to affirm X and to maintain that it is not causally influencing/influenced by Y (when in fact it is).

"To abstract is to focus on aspects of something whilst not assuming the non-existence, or non-impact, of features not focused explicitly upon (that are abstracted from). To isolate theoretically is precisely to treat those aspects not focused upon as non-existent, or at least as sealed off, as having no systematic influence" (see Fullbrook, 2008, p. 203).

Second, Lawson relates the conceptual couple "mechanical – non-mechanical" with the pair "abstraction – isolation". And he seems to think that abstraction is valid in both cases, but "isolation" is only valid when it is performed within a mechanical field.

"...clearly abstraction, but not theoretical isolation, will be relevant wherever the whole is not just the mechanical sum of parts..." (see Fullbrook, 2008, p. 204).

The decision about how the world is has priority over the chosen method. Of course, how the world "really is" is an arguable matter. If this interpretation is correct, Lawson largely agrees with the argument of Cartwright just exposed. But as their theoretical frames are considerably different it is not easy to set the limits of their agreements. Cartwright, for example, emphasizes the qualitative diversity of the members of non-mechanics wholes, which would inhibit the use of the analytical method within these domains; Lawson, however, seems to think that the organic totalities (wholes) are essentially composed by relations that cannot be untied by analysis. Lawson's argument hinges on the kind of relations among the elements of a totality, not the qualitative character of the elements themselves.

Third, when X and Y form a totality one of them cannot be isolated without dismantling the resulting total organization. Most of the social or economic entities are *totalities* (i.e., wholes containing parts *internally* related). For example, the family, as object of study (the family relations), conforms such a totality, since it is not appropriate to study the net of parental relations examining separately the behavior of each of its members.

Fourth, another way, perhaps clearer, to appreciate Lawson's view is to notice that the pertinence of theoretical isolation depends on its compliance with extremely restrictive conditions: it must be *materially* possible to perform a *physical* isolation within the intended target. Laboratory experiments constitute paradigmatic cases of physical isolations, in which the causal influence of certain factors over their effects are nullified.

This throws more light on what Lawson considers one of the central tasks of critical realism's approach: to take into account the ontological preconditions that would make viable (and useful) the use of "formalist" (mainstream) methods. According to Lawson, a theoretical isolation in model M comes from imagining what would happen if a physical isolation in target T (that M tries to represent) were practiced. In those cases where a physical isolation *cannot* be applied because if it were performed an organic totality would be disarticulated (the intended target will disappear), nor can theoretical isolation be legitimately practiced. One is not allowed to separate in the imagination that which cannot be separated in reality without destroying the salient characteristics of the targeted subject. Therefore, the relevance of theoretical isolations entirely depends on the viability of *physical* isolations. Given that Lawson thinks that most of the social world is made of "organic totalities", the method of isolation that conventional economic theory practices and MPE advises is mainly irrelevant.

Chapter 2
How to use the informational content of theoretical economic models

Recall that I described as "stylizations" or "stylized assumptions" any kind of alteration suffered by a representation regarding its intended target. Three sorts of stylizations can be distinguished: (a) factors which are present in the target and are incorporated within the model in a distorted form; (b) factors present in the target but are omitted within the model, and (c) factors that are inexistent in the target but are included by analytic convenience. I call them, respectively, "distortions", "omissions" and "additions". In any model omissions are inevitable and should be immune to the charge of unrealism. Models pick up some traits and leave out of consideration others. The metaphor that models are caricatures makes reference mainly to the first sort of stylizations. Both kinds of assumptions are designed with the purpose of making a contribution to an adequate representation of the intended target. Other suppositions are included, however, just to allow or facilitate the proofs given within models. I will call them *tractability* assumptions. There are two kinds of them: those that are expressed independently of the main postulates of the model (as the auxiliary assumptions in Popperian methodology), and those that adopt the form of implicit restrictions to the formulation of these postulates, as are for instance the lineal or quadratic form of a fundamental equation that describes the behavior of a set of economic factors. To illustrate, the fundamental relation $C = f(Y)$ may be expressed as $C = (a + bY)$. The linear expression may be included not because it is meant to find the true causal relation of both factors in our world, but just because it is easier or more convenient to connect C and Y in this form.

Regarding tractability assumptions, the reproach of unrealism is sound and methodologically useful. Their presence makes it difficult to defend a model's external validity, particularly how to use the knowledge provided under these conditions in real market economies. In connection with this, two types of solutions have been proposed. The first, which we call "internalist", argues that certain operations carried out within models (i.e., inside the realm of what Sugden calls the "model world"), particularly derivational robustness analysis, may show a model's epistemic value[1]. "Externalist" solutions, on the other hand, argue that in order to acquire epistemic relevance economic models have to be supplemented with some kind of external knowledge. In the following sections five different strategies to support some of these views will be examined: (a) the interpretation of models as parables (Cartwright); (b) the suggestion that what is needed is to train suitable interpreters (Colander), (c)) the concept of models as open formulas (Alexandrova), (d) Sugden's view about credible models. Despite their differences, all of these views are based on the assumption that economic models including gross mismatches with their intended targets as well as arbitrary tractability assumptions, may contain after all reliable and relevant knowledge about our world. The problem, according to these views, is that such knowledge is not directly usable: the applicability of economic models to situations of our world crucially depends on the assistance of some kind of background knowledge coming from outside the models themselves.

1. Externalist solutions

1.1 Cartwright's vision of models as parables

As seen above, Cartwright (1999, 2007a, 2007b) called attention to the problem of the "overconstraint" suffered by economic models of the "analogue economies" type, which generated a trade-off between their internal and external validity. In a more recent paper (Cartwright, 2008) she offers a new interpretation and argues that the trade-off may not take place after all. To reach this conclusion she contrasts two ways of understanding

---

[1] Derivational robustness analysis, as understood by Kuorikoski, Lehtinen and Marchioni (2010), replaces the comparison between a model and its intended target by the comparison between different versions of a basically identical model. The strategy is to build a family of models and claim that the derivational robustness analysis allows identifying existing causal connections in our world simply by comparing among each of the members of the family.

economic models: as fables and as parables. She argues that fables deliver a "message" or "lesson" that is explicitly formulated within the text. Parables, however, yield (or perhaps it would be better to say "suggest") a lesson that is not contained in the model itself, but must somehow be built from the outside taking into account relevant portions of available background knowledge. This means that models can have a "correct" lesson within them, but it must be partly construed out of the materials provided by the model on the basis of theoretical and extra theoretical knowledge. Models deliver a lesson that despite being abstract in nature may be applicable to the specific economies of our world. Her vision of models as parables can be understood as a new strategy in the broad project of mainstream philosophy of economics intended to "recovering the practice" of mainstream model building.

Cartwright's new vision is consistent with an idea that she has advanced before (see for instance Cartwright, 2007b): economic models do provide valuable informative content, and if there is any doubt about what their epistemic relevance is, the problem lies not in the models themselves, but in our difficulties for developing *another* type of knowledge able to reveal *how to use* the model's information. This is precisely what happens with parables. To identify their "lessons" and be able to apply them to situations of our world the use of background knowledge is crucially required. Her defense of the epistemic relevance of economic models whose results depend on the discretionary addition of tractability assumptions is unconvincing, however. Let me mention some problems of this vision.

(1) There is no guarantee that such models will deliver a "correct" abstract lesson (i.e., a lesson applicable to the real world). On the other hand, even if models contain materials for building the right lessons out of them, there are no rules for identifying them unequivocally. Besides, the lessons that models could suggest, being dependent on the particular state of knowledge which prevails at the moment, may vary according to times and places, and are always subject to revision.

(2) The lessons and applications that models facilitate are no longer based on the *consequences* obtained from the model but on other, more abstract content, which is not deduced from the model, but is "inferred"

or "captured" otherwise. Arguably, then, the problem of overconstraint is not resolved, but is rather diluted by changing the reference point: the *consequences* are still over-constrained (since Cartwright is not advocating a change in models, but in their interpretation), but now the focus is placed not on them (or their applicability), but in *lessons* which supposedly do not depend on the set of tractability assumptions.

(3) To spread their message, parables do not need to deliver rigorous proofs, and much less employ advanced math or heroic idealizations. In fact, it seems that the "lessons" that economic models offer could be obtained without having to impose deductive power within the model by adding strategic tractability assumptions. Why do modelers send messages or lessons through analogue economies? If the epistemic value of models resides at a more abstract level, what is the purpose of over-constraining their results (often with a huge amount of tractability assumptions)? It seems that a more informal argumentation would be enough (and surely the lesson so delivered would be clearer).

(4) A potential problem of Cartwright's shift from methodology and epistemology to literary analysis is that parables, as many everyday sayings, are not only ambiguous in their content, but frequently suggest opposite lessons that contradict each other. One can then choose the lesson that best suits his interests or the particular occasion. This pliability of the parables could certainly explain the ease with which applications for economic models are found and their epistemic relevance taken as granted. I can't tell whether this plasticity should count as a credit or a defect.

1.2. Interpreting economic models

In his article "The economics profession, the financial crisis, and method", David Colander focused his analysis on the performance of "the dominant dynamic stochastic general equilibrium macroeconomics model" (DSGE) regarding the global financial crisis of 2007-2008. This crisis was so deep that "the world economy came perilously close to a systemic failure in which a financial system collapse almost undermined the entire world economy as we know it" (Colander, 2010, p. 1). In this case his analysis refers not to "analogue economies", but to a type of model designed to be applied to a particular situation of our economic system. It is then interesting to see how its performance is evaluated. Colander holds a moderate position, pointing out, like Cartwright did regarding analogous economies, that such a model has valuable information about the world which deserves to be considered and elaborated.[2]

As usual only shortcomings are explicitly mentioned. In this regard he argues that those who were looking at the world through DSGE's lenses were prevented from seeing that conditions for the advent of the crisis were growing inside the economy, despite that "the possibility that a crisis might occur at some point was becoming evident to many observers". To some degree one could excuse this failure pointing out that after all predictions are usually unattainable in economics. But Colander emphasizes a rather different point. He asserts that "it did not take a rocket economist to recognize problems in the financial sector as the burgeoning sub-prime mortgage market was bringing in less creditworthy buyers. At some point, that process of credit expansion had to end". This observation seems to imply that those who did *not* have the help of DSGE's analytical tools had a *more clear* perception of the situation than those who counted with the model's help. Leaving aside the difficulties of anticipating future events, the fact remains that this model has also been useless to *analyze and understand* the crisis *once it was already present*.

The inadequacy of the model for examining the crisis is explained by the purpose of simplifying its object of analysis, which exhibits a substantial complexity. To be tractable

> "...the DSGE model ruled out meaningful considerations of the financial crises by its representative agent and global rationality assumptions".

Colander does not have much hope in the strict adherence to this strategy. In his opinion:

---

[2] As he says, the criticism that DGS has received "does not mean that such abstract modeling should not be done. We strongly supported such basic research" (Colander, 2010, p.421).

"mathematical modelers should deal with that complexity head on, rather than focus on models that assume much of that complexity away as we believed the dominant dynamic stochastic general equilibrium (DSGE) macroeconomics model did" (Colander, 2010, p.1).

Consequently, Colander rejects the ongoing practice of working on models like the DSGE and advocates for developing more sophisticated models, which are characterized as "highly complex heterogeneous agent, coordination failure models that might have been able to incorporate such events as a crisis of confidence". It could be thought that this (forthcoming) new generation of highly complex models would finally meet the requirement of epistemic relevance. However, Colander admits that future models *will not provide a firm basis for the implementation of successful economic policies* either. As he points out, "models of complex systems do not, and at our current stage of knowledge, cannot, provide definite policy answers - they simply provide guidance to individuals who have real-world experience and a detailed knowledge of the institutional structure".

Colander's view is convergent with the ones offered by other authors that we examine in this chapter, like Nancy Cartwright and Ana Alexandrova, in the sense that they all believe that standard economic models do provide some type of useful and enlightening knowledge, even if this knowledge is not directly linked to situations of our world. Therefore, in all these cases the relevant question is *how that knowledge should be used to obtain practical results and build successful economic policies*. What distinguishes Colander's views from other opinions is the nature of the proposed solutions, which consist in this case in academic and attitudinal changes.

First, economists are advised to assume more responsibility when the properties and results of the DSGE model are communicated outside the narrow community of experts and model builders. Particularly, published models should include "an explicit warning directed at the non-scientific users of the model. This warning could include a list of what the researchers see as limiting assumptions of the model, and the researchers' beliefs about whether the model can be used to guide policy" (Colander, 2010, p. 424)

Still more important is his indication that expertise in the use of macroeconomic models requires practical knowledge of the economy as well as other kinds of knowledge and skills, which are different from that involved in the practice of modeling. In particular, Colander proposes a crucial institutional shift, which consists in allocating public funds for training economists in the interpretation of models with a view to their applications.

> "Currently, most economists are not selected for their ability to, or trained in how to, 'choose' an appropriate model, or otherwise relate a model to policy. Doing this requires knowledge of a wide range of models, historical knowledge, and institutional knowledge. They are trained almost entirely to produce models. The other ability they must learn on their own. By design graduate training has eliminated those courses, such as the history of economic thought, methodology, economic history, or courses surveying literature, that are most relevant for training students to choose among, and interpret models...A potential solution to this problem is to increase the number of researchers trained in interpreting models rather than developing models. This would mean viewing the interpretation of models as a separate skill from producing models. If a funding agency were to provide research grants specifically to interpret models, that problem could be somewhat alleviated. In a sense, what I am suggesting is the creation of an applied science subdivision of the National Science Foundation's social science division. This subdivision would fund research on the usefulness and interpretation of models" (Colander, 2010, pp. 425-426).

Colander's proposal is original and interesting, but somewhat understates and dilutes the role which, according to mainstream philosophy of economics, models play in the production of relevant and reliable knowledge about the specific economies. Colander's perspective makes the potential usefulness of this knowledge heavily dependent on the acquisition of other kinds of knowledge whose source and legitimacy was originally contested. In fact, Mill, Senior and many other economists of the past claimed that economic theory was scientific in the sense that it went well beyond the knowledge of economic affairs available to ordinary people, historians of economics and entrepreneurs. But it seems that Colander's perspective re-enhances the role of the very kinds of knowledge that were thought superseded by economics' theoretical practice.

1.3. Technological use of economic models. Towards a more applied economics

Recently, Ana Alexandrova has defended a new vision about the role that economic models play in the implementation of economic policies. She limits her analysis to one particular model, the auction model, which is praised as a paradigmatic case of successful application in the design of institutions (Alexandrova, 2008; Alexandrova and Northcott, 2008). Her purpose is to explain what its contribution is in the achievement of this goal. She argues that the main existing rival views about models' applicability are not useful in this case. Alexandrova's approach is a promising way to defend the practical relevance of economic models, suggesting, at the same time, a more general way to appreciate what exactly the applicability of models that incorporate tractability assumptions depends on.

Economic models can be used to represent (and be applied to) a certain target T. According to Alexandrova, there are two main views that seek to give an account of their applicability: the "satisfaction of assumption" account, which is attributed to Daniel Hausman, and the "capacity account" developed by Nancy Cartwright. According to them, a model represents (and is applicable to) T when, respectively, its assumptions are satisfied in T or the causes described in it occur in T. To illustrate her position, let's express it in Hausman' concept: If a model M contains assumptions, some of which are idealizations (we read: tractability assumptions), this fact prevents them from being strictly true in T. But in that case, according to Hausman, it is possible to gradually de-idealize those assumptions until they match the relevant characteristics of the "intended target". De-idealization allows models to be applicable and to acquire empirical content.

How to use the informational content of theoretical economic models

Alexandrova (2006, p. 183) points out that this strategy is only possible in some cases because it is not always possible to de-idealize the tractability assumptions incorporated into a model. She says, for instance,

> "In what sense is it more realistic for agents to have discretely as opposed to continuously distributed valuations? It is controversial enough to say that people form their beliefs about the value of the painting or the profit potential of an oil well by drawing a variable from a probability distribution. So the further question about whether this distribution is continuous or not is not a question that seems to make sense when asked about human bidders and their beliefs."

Her proposal is then intended to "recover" the practice of model building in those cases in which de-idealization cannot be followed. She tries to give an account of how, despite this limitation, economic models can be applied successfully to obtain desired economic institutions and practical results. To examine her vision let me describe a model M in this sketchy way:

Given C1, ... Cn, a certain characteristic F causes behavior B   (1)

A more synthetic way of expressing its content is

"Under conditions C, F causes B"   (1')

Note that M is a *closed* formula, in the sense that all of its assumptions are specified. But one thing is the model and another thing is its use. Alexandrova points out that M can be *used to build a hypothesis* in which only *some* of its assumptions (or *none* of them) is specified. The hypothesis has this form:

Under conditions X
(that *may or may not* include conditions C), F causes B   (2)

In (2), C has a purely notional presence, since it may be completely undetermined. For this reason she proposes considering models as *open formulas*. Strictly speaking, the content of (2) boils down to the following:

(In our world)
There are conditions X, where F causes B   (2')

In (2') F and B are conditions whose properties are known and X is the unknown variable whose "values" have to be found. Interestingly, the original model, which suggests the hypothesis (2) and (2'), does not provide any clue for discovering those values. In fact, the model itself contains no hypotheses such as those made in (2) or (2'). They are independent from the model, though inspired by it. From this point of view the model has no real world informative content of its own: it is rather considered as a source of hints, tools and resources for generating hypotheses about the world. In Alexandrova's words the auction model functions as a "framework or heuristic for formulating hypotheses".

But how workable is such heuristic? Is it really a form of heuristic after all? Suppose that "B" is a desirable outcome and "F" is a state of things which we can implement in reality. Suppose then that a model M proves that under conditions C, F causes B. C describes a set of conditions that are logically *sufficient* to ensure such an outcome. The epistemic significance (relevance) of the model seems to depend strongly on the feasibility of conditions C. What is then accomplished by rigorously proving that "F causes B" if it is obtained at the expense of introducing arbitrary assumptions, which supposedly describe a situation that is absent in real economic environments? It seems that such a proof contributes nothing to identify what conditions should be found or created in *our world* to get B guaranteeing F. We are in a situation that seems to be very close to that of the logical exercise outlined above.

In circumstances like these the technological moment comes to occupy the center stage in Alexandrova's account[3]. Starting from (2') that ensures that

---

[3] It is important to be clear about the particular type of laboratory experiment that concerns Alexandrova. Her analysis focused exclusively on the role of experimentation regarding *technological applications*, not for the purpose of testing

there are (unspecified) conditions out of which "F causes B", economists with practical orientation (and a host of other skillful people) can get hands to work and try to find out concrete conditions C* (other than C), that can be implemented in our world and have the property that once imposed make F result in B. In fact, the main claim of Alexandrova is that this achievement has already been obtained with remarkable success in the case of the auction model. Maybe Alexandrova is right on this point, but since in her account models merely inspire (2') and do that in an extremely vague form, there remains the philosophical problem of assessing what exactly auction models' contribution is to the solution of the question raised by the hypothesis. Did the economic engineers referred in Alexandrova's account need rigorous proof like the one provided by the model to find particular conditions C* under which, doing F, B is obtained in our world? Did they find, at least, a clue in the model to imagine the specific content of the set C*?

If "F causes B" is a desirable conclusion, there seem to be two different research programs concerning this result. One mathematical (logical): search for *any* conditions C under which the result could be deduced. Another, practical: find conditions C* feasibly implemented in our world such that the production of F leads to B. Unless a clear connection between both programs can be exhibited (something that Alexandrova's paper fails to show) to get busy building models diverts resources from the technological approach of directly "building" in practice the desired result. This construction, it seems, does not need at all any of the solutions offered within the model.

---

models as this activity is usually understood. This is why she distinguishes between "test" and "testbed". The test of a model is to create or find a situation in which that model's assumptions are met, and see if their results are also obtained. In a testbed, on the other hand, it is known or supposed that the assumptions of the model are *not* satisfied. Its purpose is to obtain the same results obtained within the model from different or additional conditions than those referred to in the model. Alexandrova's testbeds enhance the role of applied economics and the autonomy of the achieved results regarding the particular conditions described in models. Testbeds are better described as a practice performed by economic engineers rather than by experimental economists in the traditional sense of the term.

1.4. Credible models

Representation involves a sort of similarity between the features insulated within a model and those present in its intended target, a deeply problematic proposition. Another way for approaching the problem of how to think the link between theoretical models with their target in real economies is setting aside the basic concept of similarity and put in use the concept of *plausibility* (or some other concept akin with this). This is the way chosen by Sugden. If an acceptable way of stating that a model M whose target is T is *plausible* or *credible* regarding T (Sugden prefers this last word) could be found, it may be used to state when and why it is legitimate to extrapolate to T what has been discovered within M.

Sugden (2000) distinguishes among the "real world" (W) and the world of theoretical representations, or "model world" (M). In his view those worlds that are described within models are "parallel" to our ordinary world of economic events, in the sense that they have been built in an independent way.

> "On this view, the model is not so much an abstraction from reality as a parallel reality. The model world is not constructed by starting with the real world and stripping out complicating factors: although the model world is *simpler* than the real world, the one is not a *simplification* of the other" (Sugden, 2000, p. 25).

Nevertheless this could be extremely useful according to Sugden. Let's see why. Suppose that we know that a definite pattern R of economic events exists in W. The question about the cause of R in W may be answered by building a model M in which the variable X designs (describes the main features of) R, and X is implied by a set of premises C. In this case, under *some conditions* we are legitimated to conjecture that C (which is a set of sufficient conditions for obtaining X) describe the causal mechanisms that generate R in W. What Sugden offers is a typical explanation of the "what could make R possible" form. He invites us to believe that this approach helps to explain the appeal that Akerlof (1970) and Shelling's (1971) models have for us.

How to use the informational content of theoretical economic models

The next step is clarifying what are the special conditions that make it legitimate to extrapolate to W that which is found in M. Or, more precisely, what allows us to explain pattern R present in W invoking the mechanism C which has been successful in order to entail X within M. Sugden's solution is simple and compelling in my view: we may say that there is a mechanism (whose main features are described in C) causing R in W as long as C is *credible*. He offers two main attempts for clarifying "credibility".

The first one is close to one of the last of Cartwright's defenses of the usefulness of economic models. He approaches models with the tools of *literary analysis* and grounds credibility on some kind of intuitive (pre-model) knowledge already available.

> "Credibility in models is, I think, rather like credibility in 'realistic' novels. In a realistic novel, the characters and locations are imaginary, but the author has to convince us that they are credible – that there could be people and places like those in the novel. ...We judge the author has failed if we find a person acting out of character, or if we find an anachronism in a historical novel: these are things that *couldn't* have happened" (Sugden, 2000, p. 25).

Isahia Berlin (1966) has used a similar position for distinguishing between good and bad historiography. According to him good historians are endowed with an especial *don* that he referred to as *historical sense*, which is a capacity for acknowledging some particular order among different elements of a totality. They are successful integrating features of the whole picture that plain people see as independent or separate. Historical sense guides good historians in the use of some key notions like *typical* or *anachronic*. For instance, even if there are two main ways in which a sentence may be anachronic, one of them is rather superficial and alludes to the fact that the feature attributed to a particular epoch has taken place on another occasion (what is asserted is in fact false). A second use of the term is deeper and more interesting: it refers to a situation in which an event did not occur as a matter of fact. For instance, if someone said that Hamlet was (or could have been) written inside the court of Gengis Khan in outer Mongolia he would be asserting not only a false statement, but something that is absurd. Such a thing not only did not occur; it could not have happened. And this judgment is true even if we lack any kind of empirical evidence about this. Berlin emphasizes that anybody can see that this pretense is false in the first sense of the term, but only good historians acknowledge that it is ridiculous. This second notion of anachronism remits to the coherence of the parts that constitute the whole. Having historical sense means to be endowed with the capacity for integrating, for seeing which thing goes with which thing (Berlin, 1966, p. 29).

Going back to Sugden, to characterize credibility by means of literary tools is suggestive, but he notes that "the reader will expect more than analogy", so that "the obvious question that I have to answer is: What constitutes credibility in economic models?". He offers two criteria for credibility. The first one is internal coherence, not in the sense of logical consistency, whose importance is taken as granted, but in a more "material" sense which refers to contents.

> "The assumptions of a good model (must) cohere in the broader sense that they fit naturally together". For instance, a model cannot mix hypothesis of "hyper-rationality" in one context and "bounded rationality" in another. This sort of coherence is needed for credibility: "If a model lacks coherence, its results cannot be seen to follow naturally from a clear conception of how the world might be; this prompts the suspicion that the assumptions have been cobbled together to generate predetermined results" (Sugden, 2000, p. 26).

The second credibility requirement goes beyond *internal* coherence (one which is restricted to the parts inside the model) and involves the relation between the model-world and reality. He asserts that models:

> "must also cohere with what is known about causal processes in the real world. Thus, Akerlof's assumptions that prices tend to their market-clearing levels is justified by evidence from a wide range of 'natural' and laboratory markets. Schelling's assumptions that many people have at

least mildly segregationist preferences is justified by psychological and sociological evidence, and coheres with common intuition and experience" (Sugden, 2000, p. 26).

In my view Sugden's position is not completely consistent. On the one hand, he tries hard to avoid being enrolled in the isolationist view which in addition to the objections already examined in the previous chapter faces severe difficulties in elucidating some of its key notions, like representation and similarity (resemblance). But in so doing he asserts that modeling in economics is like creating imaginary or "parallel" worlds, going too close to an autonomist vision of economic models.

However, Sugden's position may be also interpreted in a manner that is opposite to the one he explicitly defends. He seems to believe that models are produced following this sequence: first a parallel reality is forged (which is simpler than its target and independent of it), then the desired pattern R is deductively obtained from a set of postulates C within the model, and finally as long as C is found credible (plausible as a causal mechanism able to operate in the real target T) some explanatory power is attributed to the model: it provides information about how market economies *could* work. I feel disappointed with this description. In my view (which ultimately is more consistent with Berlin and Sugden's literary approaches) what happens is that it is the use of already available knowledge (presumably provided by a mix of observation, experience of life, other social disciplines and common sense) what introduces credibility in the model. The kinds of models to which Sugden refers are constructed as credible *ex-professo* (selecting from reality only those features of markets and agents that we know exist or may exist in real markets). The story that we first build any model some way (a parallel reality) and then surprisingly we find the model credible may be attractive only if one is trying to escape from the problems of the isolation view.

Sugden's perspective sides with that of the many authors who assign a central role to background knowledge (one which comes from common sense or has been produced by other social disciplines), granting epistemic relevance to economic models. More importantly, Sugden draws up a demarcation inside the model world, distinguishing between "credible" models, that provide useful suggestions to us about the operation of the markets, and those that are useless to this purpose (and whose epistemic value remains rather shady).

In contradistinction with a majority of mainstream philosophers of economics who assume the defense of any model backed by disciplinarian recognition, Sugden adopts a refreshing critical perspective. Talking about incoherent models (those that violate his first criteria of credibility) he says that "ad hoc models of this kind may be commonplace in economic journals, but if they are, that does not justify them" (p. 26). Those models that are not coherent with what we know about our world (his second criterion) deserve in my view even less justification.

Summing up, the distinction between credible and non-credible models is important and deserves to be taken into account and to be developed. In my view, only the first kind of models should be invested with epistemic relevance. Nevertheless, in spite of their merits credible models do not seem to be more than a clarification, ordering and systematization of practical and ordinary knowledge already available. It is not easy to find realized in them the promise – announced more than two centuries ago – of a rigorously scientific economic theory able to surpass and replace the views of entrepreneurs and ordinary men.

2. "Internalist" solutions: Derivational Robustness Analysis (DRA)

2.1 Introduction

The aptitude of conventional economic models for explaining or helping to understand economic phenomena as well as their capacity to serve as a base for the implementation of economic policies has been questioned because of their discretional use of tractability suppositions. Against these objections it has been claimed that a type of robustness analysis (Derivational Robustness Analysis – DRA), which is frequently used in economics may be applied to avoid this problem and prove to be relevant for epistemic purposes. If true, this claim would be important for two reasons:

(a) because it is a form of defense of conventional models that apparently operate without the use of background knowledge or any other sort of extra-model knowledge, which as seen before is usually invoked to justify their applicability;

(b) because voices like Alexandrova's, who advocate for an "economic engineering", DRA can be interpreted as a plea in favor of a "pure" theoretical practice, which supposedly has epistemic relevance by itself. In this section we will criticize this strategy, which has been defended recently by KLM (2010) and KL (2009).

Derivational Robustness Analysis (DRA) should not be confused with other forms of robustness analysis with which it shares some characteristics. DRA constructs a family of arguments (models) which have in common some key fixed suppositions, called *substantive assumptions* (SA), whereas others suppositions, called *auxiliary assumptions* (AA) change from one model to another one. What DRA is supposed to determine is whether a certain result R may be obtained in all the models of the family in spite of the changes in AA. Its basic structure is:

SA
AAj

R

Where SA remains constant and AA is replaced successively by diverse variants AA1, AA2,...., etc. If, in spite of these changes, R continues to be a consequence of the different sets of premises, it is said that R is robust respect to SA.

2.2 Basic KLM's presupposition for approaching DRA

The above schematic representation of DRA presupposes the fulfillment of the following key condition:[4]

---

[4] Hausman (1992) uses a similar scheme although in reference to a context of test in which (a) main and auxiliary suppositions were represented separately and (b) auxiliary assumptions were less reliable than the first ones.

(1) Separation between SA and AA.

Nowhere is this supposition developed in detail in KLM (2010). It does not seem to be easily defensible, nevertheless, although it is essential for the development of the theses that the authors wish to expose. The separation between SA and AA is a central point in KLM's approach, which at first sight seems to be a particular case of the more traditional distinction between main and auxiliary hypotheses. Within the framework of traditional methodology they were considered as two sets of *logically independent* hypotheses. Nevertheless, this kind of separation is hard to sustain in the case of DRA. As the authors emphasize, in the most interesting cases the substantive suppositions do not have a pure content, separated from the form in which they are represented: they must acquire *some form* (generally mathematical) at the very moment of being formulated. This explains why the shared core of substantial suppositions in the family of models occurs necessarily associated to some tractability suppositions.

> "Tractability requirements sometimes demand that substantial assumptions are also incorporated in ways that are more specific than desired: the causal factors making up the core mechanism have to be implemented in the model in some mathematical form" (KLM, 2010, p. 10).

For analytical purposes however a clear split between SA and AA may be established. For example, suppose that SA is "Q depends on L" (i.e., "production depends on work"). Such qualitative expression does not serve the purpose of obtaining the sort of rigorous proofs aimed at in DRA, and for this reason it is necessary to re-express it into some mathematical form. For example, "$Q = f(a + bL)$" or some other defined formal expression. But now the original SA and the particular form in which now it has been invested are conflated. As long as each model of the family incorporates SA under some relatively sophisticated mathematical form picked up to allow desired demonstrations, SA and AA are indistinguishable within the framework of DRA, and their attempted separation collapses.

In what follows, we are going to overlook this problem, which actually affects the possibility of implementing the set of conditions demanded by DRA in the

How to use the informational content of theoretical economic models

KLM version. We will concentrate our attention in examining if an analytical frame like the one provided by the authors (assuming it were constructible and applicable), allows them to obtain their aimed goals.

2.3 The epistemic relevance of DRA

KLM maintain that DRA has epistemic relevance, meaning that it contributes to knowledge. This can be understood in two ways. The first, not controversial, is that the family of arguments unfolded in DRA has the capacity to show that at least some of the AA, that at first sight someone could have believed were (logically) necessary for obtaining R, can be replaced by other auxiliary suppositions that allow us to reach the same consequence. For example, if it were presumed at first that set AA1 was a necessary condition for the deduction of R, DRA can show that other sets of auxiliary suppositions, AA2, AA3, etc., when conjoined with SA are equally sufficient for the derivation of R.

But KLM goes beyond this rather trivial point. They wish to defend a stronger and more interesting thesis: they maintain that DRA offers relevant *causal* information about real markets (our world). This claim is however controversial. As the authors have indicated, "Robert Sugden argues that robustness analysis cannot play an epistemic role in grounding model-world relationships because the procedure is only a matter of comparing models with each other" (KLM, 2008). Besides, they also acknowledge that "Woodward claims that derivational robustness does not provide any additional epistemic credence to the conclusion". They admit that "if he were right, a significant portion of theoretical model building in economics would have no epistemic value" (KLM, 2010).

The central goal of KLM (2010) is to refute these assertions. To do that, the authors take for granted the validity of two new assumptions:

> (2) Existence of an epistemic asymmetry between SA and AA. The first ones are assumed as true and the second as false. In a weaker version it is said that we have greater confidence in the truth of the first than in the truth of the second.

(3) Such asymmetry is founded on Background Knowledge (BK), which supposedly enjoys consensus from the discipline and is available before DRA is practiced.

Taken together, both suppositions allow KLM to claim that SA describes causal factors or mechanisms operating in real markets. SA is presumably true, or at least non-problematic, acquiring its legitimacy from a given and non-controversial BK. AA, however, involves false suppositions, which diverge from reality affecting the results that are reached by reasoning from them. It is doubtful then that the epistemic asymmetry of both sets of assumptions can be asserted if an explicit distinction between them (that incorporates two disjoint subgroups of assumptions in the model) is lacking.

2.4 Confiability of DRA's inferences

KLM's reconstruction of DRA may be clarified by changing the terms by which they approach the issue and pointing out that the content of SA comes, so to speak, from two different levels. Some of its content comes from the underlying qualitative relation involved in SA. For example, "monetary emission creates inflation". This qualitative content is assumed to be known. But some additional content comes to SA from the form that this expression adopts when expressed within the model. This additional content is admittedly false. Described at a qualitative level, SA is assumed to be true. Described more accurately, under some particular mathematical form, it may be plainly incorrect. A suggestive way to express this is that SA is a complex formulation that consists of a qualitative content (which is credible as long as it is endorsed by BK), and a more precise content (imposed on it by a particular formulation which is false or has little credibility). Both aspects of SA contribute to reach the robust results.

If the aimed at consequences R of SA could be derived at a general level all would be fine. R would be as true as SA at that level. But as long as it is also implied by the particular content of SA, which is imposed by its mathematical form, its truth-value remains uncertain. So one problem that the authors must confront regards the trustworthiness of the consequences obtained in these conditions. They express this problem in two diverse ways:

How to use the informational content of theoretical economic models

a) The inference derived from premises that contain false statements is not reliable;
b) The truth of the results obtained in these conditions (or the belief thereof that R exists in real markets) is suspicious.

KLM (2010) make the strong claim that DRA will fortify our conviction in the trustworthiness of the inference that leads to R, and would increase our confidence that R exists in the real world. Let us see if they manage to reach these goals satisfactorily. They provide two different arguments.

First. Suppose the truth of that portion of the content of SA that is located at a general level is beyond question. An unobjectionable way to increase the confidence in the inferences made by means of DRA would be to replace progressively those particular formulations of SA suspected to be false by other ones believed true. If DRA allows them to keep obtaining R as a consequence, this very fact would increase the confidence that the inference deduced by DRA leads to the truth, just because R depends less and less on false suppositions. But the authors concede that such a strategy cannot be attainable. In fact, they note that "it may not be possible to measure how 'far' from the truth any given assumption is". Although their argument implies that sometimes this estimation *could* be possible, the authors do not elaborate on this aspect, which could have been used in their defense of the epistemic value of DRA. They instead state that all the AA involve falsehood. These conditions cast doubts about the possibility that DRA could make a contribution to fortify the trustworthiness of the inferences made within the family of models. At least, the strategy just indicated cannot be put in practice.

Is it possible to find a way to improve the confidence in the inferences even if they keep depending on the use of *false* premises? Apparently not: if the successive substitutions made by DRA consist in changing certain AA believed to be false by other AA that are as suspicious as the previous ones, it is difficult to see in what sense the whole procedure improves the trustworthiness of the inferences that can be made in each round from the new premises (that is to say, in what sense can be said that the new inference is more reliable than the previous one).

Second. KLM think they can avoid the inconvenience by not focusing on the falsehood (*in toto*) of AA, and shifting to the claim that what really matters is the *particular* falsehood involved in any of them and the amount of distortion that the involved falsehood of each AA can generate in the consequences of the argument.

> "...what really interests us is whether a particular deviation from the truth matters for a given result or not. Robustness analysis helps in assessing this question by providing information on whether or not the particular falsity exhibited by some assumption is responsible for a given modeling result". [5]

The idea seems to be this. Assume that AA1 is a set of particular formulations of SA believed to be false, and M is a model in which the qualitative truth involved (embedded) in SA in conjunction with AA1 leads deductively to R. If, in conjunction with SA, R could be obtained by substituting AA1 for another set of auxiliary hypothesis AA2 (which can be also false but in a different sense in which AA1 is false), would this count like a proof that the *particular falsehood* contained in AA1 is irrelevant for the obtaining of R? [6]

If, as it was analyzed above, claiming that AA1 is "irrelevant" means merely that it is not a necessary (logical) condition for the derivation, KLM would be right. But this point is beyond question from the start!

---

[5] From this perspective DRA shows that auxiliary suppositions, taken one by one, are logically irrelevant for the deduction of R. That is to say, that R could also be derived in the model by replacing those suppositions for others similarly convenient. This allows KLM to maintain that the epistemic value of DRA lies in that it allows identifying which of those factors that a priori were assumed to be irrelevant in the generation of R, really are irrelevant and which are not. This way, the kind of knowledge that DRA provides is information about the necessary and sufficient conditions for the derivation of a given consequence.

[6] "...the way in which substantial assumptions are implemented in the model may introduce an element of falsehood, which is hoped to have little consequence for the result" (KLM, 2010).

2.5 Causal relevance

Let's go back to causality. KLM try to make a *causal* (not merely logical) reading of DRA. For that reason they jump to the conclusion that AA1 is *causally* irrelevant. Going even further with their idea of reading as causal connections that are strictly deductive, KLM seem to think that the *causal irrelevance* (of AAi respect to R) can be an indicator of the causal *relevance* of SA with respect to R. The idea now seems to be this: as long as it can be shown that the successive auxiliary suppositions are causally irrelevant respect to R, the confidence that SA is causally relevant respect to it grows. I think they are wrong. However, the relation between deductive and causal connections seems to be far more complex. As Cartwright argued, deductive chains do not always follow the line of the causes.

If, in principle, there were infinite ways to model the tractability of a given set of substantive suppositions (AA1, AA2 ..... AAn ......), to show that AA1 is not necessary for the derivation of R, this proves nothing about the problem that is approached by KLM: if there indeed is a causal relation between SA (taken at its qualitative level) and R. The situation is still worse. If AA1 and AA2 were the only two ways to impose tractability to a set of suppositions SA, and DRA were successful in obtaining R from SA eliminating first AA1 and then AA2, this exercise would either prove nothing about the (supposedly causal) relation that SA and R maintain to each other. Remember that one of the main ideas of KLM is to infer causal relations from deductive relations. But the fact is that SA by itself does not imply R. What such an exercise would prove is that SA in conjunction with AA1 *or* AA2 implies R. If KLM wanted to prove that SA is *causally* relevant with respect to R (assuming the shaky claim that deduction indicates causation), it would have to accomplish a completely different exercise of robustness: to show that there is *no way* of proving R if the qualitative content of SA is not included among the premises of the models. I do not know how a similar proof could be obtained, but certainly KLM do not offer it; and contributing to this proof is not the purpose of DRA.

2.6 Resorting to background knowledge once again

According to traditional methodology if one is interested in finding out causal relations in nature one may begin constructing a model that contains a tentative set of SA (i.e., one that describes a mechanism that presumably operates in reality), then derive results, and later implement the experimental (or observational) situation that allows to decide about SA's epistemic credentials. But KLM concede that economics faces strong restrictions when supporting empirical evidence is required and that it is difficult to expose economic models to conclusive (compelling) empirical tests.[7] Therefore KLM operate the other way around: as they take for granted that resorting to empirical evidence coming from experiments or controlled observations cannot be made without giving room to controversies, they assume that what gives support to the main postulates of economic models is already available knowledge of economic mechanisms, supposed to be adequate. I agree with this point of view, which as we have seen sooner or later arises in all the visions of the models that we have examined. But I have some doubts about the usefulness of this incorporation in order to make KLM's position stronger. Although emphasizing BK's role is an interesting point of KLM's analysis, it is not clear what it contains: common sense, practical skills, experimental knowledge, technical knowledge obtained from the rest of the social sciences? In any case, I suspect that this view spoils the whole purpose of practicing DRA, fortifying the claim that models have little (if any) use as tools for discovery.

---

[7] They affirm that it is hard to subject models to conclusive empirical tests and that even though economic models always include idealizations that turn unrealistic some of their conclusions, economic theory cannot always determine which idealizations contained in the model are crucial (and which are not) in order to achieve results. And they add that it may not always be possible to assess how close to the truth these conclusions are.

Chapter 3
Are models really necessary for theoretical practice in economics?

1. Introduction

The function that Giere and Cartwright attribute to theories and models in the construction of scientific knowledge is examined. In particular, I focus on their claim that theories are abstract formulations, and models are required to inject into them empirical content, allowing their experimental control and applications. It has been claimed that the Giere-Cartwright vision provides grounds for understanding why models are at the center of the scene from an epistemological point of view, and that such a view could also explain the role that representational models play in physics. But their view neither provides reasons to understand the role of theoretical models in economics, nor does it explain the interest that philosophers of economics have in these models. In the first place, the kind of economic models that we are considering are not the type of models that Giere and Cartwright call representational. They do not serve to make abstract formulas more concrete; they go rather in the opposite direction: they are constructions much more abstract than the current or classic speech about economic phenomena. Secondly, economic theory does not contain the sort of abstract formulations typical of hard sciences; it is better to conceive it as a much more descriptive discipline that does not require the mediation of models to refer to concrete market economies and to suggest applications and policies. Within economics theoretical models have a very different function.

2. Theories as abstract formulations. Representational models

According to Cartwright's vision, theories by themselves (a) lack empirical content and (b) need models to acquire it and become connected with reality.

> "...models are essential to theory. Without them there is just abstract mathematical structure, formulae with holes in them, bearing no relation to reality" (Cartwright, 1983, p. 159).

Particularly, she claims that models are needed for testing and applying theories. The explanation of how the connection between abstract theories and economic phenomena is successfully realized in experimental settings is based on her distinction between "interpretive" and "representative" models. Regarding this subject, Cartwright maintains that,

> "... to apply the theory to any real world situations, we need both kinds of models. We need interpretive models to exemplify how the abstract concepts of the theory apply to more concrete situations. We need representative models to represent the systems we come across in the world" (Cartwright, 2008, Reply to Morrison, p. 89).

Her perspective is analogous to Giere's position (Giere, 2004, 2008), who also conceives theories (although he prefers to speak in terms of "Principles") as abstract formulas that are applied to the phenomena by means of a succession of increasingly specific and concrete models.

For Giere, in advanced sciences models are constructed from very abstract Principles, like $F = m.a$. When examining what is the epistemological status of a similar Principle, Giere takes sides with Cartwright in that it is not an "empirical generalization" (that is to say, a universally valid law about concrete systems). In particular, $F = m.a$ does not have empirical content because what in the real world must be understood as "force" is unknown. In order to apply the Principle to concrete situations it is necessary to proceed

Are models really necessary for theoretical practice in economics?

along two steps. First, construct what he calls "interpretive models", in which several specifications of the Principle are explicitly formulated.

> "The historically most significant is the gravitational law for the force between two masses in free space, $F = Gm1m2/r2$. Others include a constant force in a uniform gravitational field, $F = -mg$, and the linear restoring force resulting in harmonic motion, $F = -kx$, where x measures the displacement from an equilibrium position" (Giere, 2008, p. 124)

Such first-round specifications of the Principle are not empirical laws yet, because they still refer to (and are exactly true within) models which are *abstract* in two senses: a) not all their concepts (like mass, force, acceleration, etc.) are completely specified; b) they do not state what real objects are the physical counterparts of their concepts. Second, in order to be able to connect interpretive models with concrete real situations one needs to construct still more specific models, what Giere calls "representative models". This can be done in diverse stages, which gives rise to a sequence of representative models like the one shown below:

Principle → Interpretative Model → Representative Model I → Representative Model II ...
$F = m.a$ $F = -g$ $h = \frac{1}{2} g t2$ $10 m = \frac{1}{2} 9.8 t2$ ...

The sequence exhibits an increasing degree of specificity. In Representative model I the body is still an ideal entity and the values of the mathematical variables remain unsettled. In the next model all the mathematical variables have been specified, but the model is still abstract because it determines the time in which an ideal (non-real) body in free fall travels ten meters. The process of growing concretization follows until arriving at a model that Giere designates as "maximally specified".[1] At this point an experiment associated to the model may be designed and the model tested. The epistemic relevance of the starting Principle ($F = m.a$) would not be revealed but for the sequence of specifications that leads to its experimental confrontation.

---

[1] Giere remarks that representative models relate "specific things in the world with elements of a model. If all relevant elements of a model are so identified the model is maximally specific" (Giere, 2010, p. 62).

Nancy Cartwright seems to agree in substance with Giere's conception. Both maintain that it is by means of this process of increasing concretization (DES-idealization or specification) via models, that theories acquire empirical content and are finally applicable to concrete situations of the real world.[2]

3. Does economics really needs mediators for approaching market economies?

This process of concretization has been successful in physics, but as was shown in chapter 2 it is not easy to apply this strategy to theoretical economic models, because frequently nobody knows how to specify some of their tractability assumptions. More importantly, even if this could be done, it seems that economics does not need theoretical models as mediators to address economic phenomena.

The question about whether economics is a science or not has become old-fashioned nowadays and it is extremely irritating to most economists. The same can be said of philosophers, because this topic belongs to the agenda of "the received" view in methodology and philosophy of science, which strives to find criteria for good science and for distinguishing science from non-science. Nevertheless, to look at the nature of scientific knowledge from a non-prescriptionist perspective can throw light on some issues that are relevant for this book. Let us consider the minimum vision of science defended by Cartwright.

> "When I talk of 'science' here I am assuming the positivist idea of exact science: science as a body of explicit knowledge, systematically organized, from which precise and unambiguous claims can be rigorously derived" (Cartwright, 2002).

On the traditional vision of science, exactitude is founded on the nature of its concepts, which refer to abstract (ideal) entities, a property that allows them

---

[2] "The paradigm is '$f = ma$.' In mechanics we do get this exact relation, but the relation we get involves an abstract concept 'force,' whose relation to the world is always mediated via some more concrete concepts" (Cartwright, 2002).

to be related to one another in an exact way. This is the Platonic vision of knowledge, which according to some interpretations was the one incorporated by Galileo in opposition to the Aristotelian perspective (Koyré, 1980). It is a conception of science perfectly compatible with Giere and Cartwright's vision, and in its minimalist formulation it hardly seems to be objectionable.

Nevertheless, in this view exactitude is obtained at the cost of losing connection with the real world. As long as the concepts are idealizations, to guarantee their connection with phenomena intermediary interpretative and representative models that gradually incorporate less and less abstract concepts are needed. To Cartwright, however, economics does not fit this vision of science. Against Menger who took for granted that "economics could be a proper science ... that uses precise concepts that have exact deductive relations among them", she pointed out that the discipline does not have abstract concepts like the ones found in physics or biology. In fact, "...much of the theorizing we do in economics right now goes exactly the opposite direction to that recommended by Menger. It uses, not abstract or theoretical or newly invented concepts – like "force", or "energy", or "electromagnetic field" – concepts partially defined by their deductive relations to other concepts, but rather, as Uskali Mäki teaches us, very mundane concepts that are unmediated in their attachment to full empirical reality" (Cartwright, 2002).

Theoretical practice in economics is then somewhat singular. Due to the semi-ordinary nature of its basic concepts, economics does not need intermediaries to refer to those phenomena in which it is interested. But this characteristic, that assures its empirical content, does not favor its pretension of being a rigorous scientific discipline. For Economy to be a science, it has to achieve this condition *in spite of* its basic concepts (not thanks to them).

It is in relation to this problem that the main function of theoretical economic models are to be understood: they are not designed to perform a mediating function, but to guarantee the scientific character of the discipline, compensating for the vagueness of its fundamental concepts. According to Cartwright, it is through the incorporation of additional suppositions to its "internal principles" that can be expressed in terms of worldly concepts, that economics obtains precision and exactitude in its results. In economics,

> "...we want our treatments to be rigorous and our conclusions to follow deductively. And the way to get deductivity when it cannot come out of the relations of the concepts is to put enough of the right kind of structure into the model" (Cartwright, 2002).[3]

The poor suitability of basic economic concepts for building precise conceptual relations is compensated by introducing other elements inside the model. The most important are tractability assumptions.

The previous sections suggest several reflections.

It is not appropriate to conceive economic (or social) theories as abstract formulas, empty of empirical content, and to see theoretical economic models as providing that content. The distinction of Gibbard and Varian between theoretical and applied models wrongly reproduces this scheme. This vision, that could be illuminating within the framework of traditional methodology, that puts at the center of its analysis the distinction between theoretical and observational terms, could still be of some aid for disciplines like physics, but not for economic theories, which refer in a rather direct way to reality.

Models like "analogous economies" involve "isolation" and typically incorporate additional suppositions that do not respond to the purpose of guaranteeing their applicability, but their tractability. The nature and role of representational models are very different from that of theoretical economic models, and typically involve an opposite conceptual movement that Mäki denominated "de-isolation".[4]

---

[3] Here "right kind of structure" does not mean "that that reproduces situations that really exist", or that are frequent and relevant in models' intended targets, but rather "that which is needed to facilitate the obtaining of precise consequences".

[4] After explaining the basic ideas of von Thunen's model Maki contrasted both approaches.
"The standard response is to say that what Thûnen has provided is just the simple 'first approximation' or some such, and it is only by way of making the model more

Are models really necessary for theoretical practice in economics?

More important for our purposes is that although both the representative models and the theoretical models of the tautologous economies type use what Cartwright designates Not-Galilean suppositions, these assumptions carry out very different functions in one case and the other: they are conditions for application (experimentation) in the first case, and conditions for the rigorous deduction of results (proofs), in the second. The epistemological consequences are different in each case. The addition of tractability Non-G suppositions (usual in theoretical economic models) generates a trade-off between extension (applicability) and rigor, something that does not occur in the case of (physics) representative models, in which the abstract theories lack extension, and the models provide it.

It can be, then, that the fundamental purpose of building theoretical models in economics is not to guarantee the test or the application of their fundamental postulates. Their main goal could rather be *logical*: to guarantee the attainment of results (consequences) in a precise and unobjectionable way. If that is the case, rather than carriers of factual information, economic models would merely be *intellectual exercises* (Birks, 2015), aimed at investigating theories (or the imaginary worlds that allegedly these theories represent), not reality.

4. Autonomist vision of models

Taking into account (a) the objections that have been advanced to "the isolationist" vision of economic models, (b) the failure of the different

---

complex and comprehensive that truth about land use can be approached. We must relax the model's idealizing assumptions one by one, thereby letting previously excluded causal factors work out their impact on the outcome, to get closer to the true representation. ... So de-isolation through de-idealization offers the only route to truth, or so the popular doctrine mentioned in the introduction goes (...) It is undeniable that such a procedure of de-isolation is needed for acquiring some interesting truths about the world. But I dispute the popular doctrine that de-isolation through de-idealization provides the only route to all possible truths. I will argue instead that Thunen's simplest model is in principle capable of delivering importantly true information about the world without de-isolation" (1992, pp. 10-11).
Leaving aside questions about truth, de-isolation is in Maki's terms what Giere and Cartwright described as a sequence of representational models that become more and more specific.

proposals designed to avoid their difficulties, (c) the problems involved in the elucidation of some key concepts like representation and similarity, which seem to be a necessary complement for a sound defense of the isolationist vision, and (d) the fact that economic theories do not need models to be connected with market phenomena, and that the use of theoretical models usually responds to a nonrepresentational purpose (i.e., the search of deductive rigor); given all these restrictions, a promissory strategy for models' believers is to emphasize their independence and autonomy. According to this vision, models are objects whose elaboration, analysis and manipulation have epistemic relevance of their own. No call for developing and improving the notion of representation and similarity, or explaining why what is said within the model makes reference to the world that surrounds us is needed. This view mixes correct insights with wrong claims. In one sense Cartwright's view is more correct than the isolationist view because conceiving models as autonomous is perfectly consistent with what most theoretical models do. Let's see why.

Correct insights. The strategy that is behind a good part of the theoretical modeling in economics is the following. If B is a result estimated as relevant and P is a set of economic principles whose validity in our world we take for granted, let us pose now to somebody this logical exercise: what other assumptions does C allow to derive B from some subgroup of P? Let us suppose that whoever exercises himself this way finds that given an arbitrary set C of suppositions, considered only for the purpose of assuring the derivation, P implies B. Here the exercise finishes. Conditions C are mere assumptions in the logical sense of the term: point of departure for the argumentation. They are what Cartwright (1983) calls suppositions of convenience, which we have designated before as suppositions of derivability or tractability.

What does this demonstration prove in reference to our world? More precisely, what is the epistemic relevance of a similar argument? If prior to its construction we thought there was no causal connection between P and B in our world, why should such a demonstration induce us to change our mind? An answer could be that C describes *plausible* conditions in our world. But by hypothesis it is assumed that this is not the case.

Consequently, this demonstration does not contribute to the credibility of the existence of a causal nexus between P and B (neither to the belief that B is a valid result in our concrete reality). It seems that we face a dilemma here. If prior to the demonstration we believe that P causally implies B, the proof does not add anything; and if the existence of a causal connection between P and B is rejected from the beginning the proof does not change things either. So, what is the contribution of a rigorous demonstration of a desired result if it is obtained at the expense of arbitrary circumstances?

An answer can be the following. The logical conjunction of premises (P. C) identifies a set of sufficient conditions for the occurrence of B. This knowledge is certainly provided by the model, and may be interesting for some people. It is rather a logical contribution, which in principle contributes nothing to the improvement of our understanding of relevant events of our world. As long as the purpose of modeling is to reach relevant and reliable empirical results, our attention is to be shifted to conditions C, particularly to its frequency (in case of happening spontaneously) or the feasibility of its implementation (if it has to be generated deliberately). If both things are discarded by hypothesis, the interest of the exercise is merely logical or theoretical. These kinds of models are intellectual exercises aimed at solving theoretical problems.

Wrong claims. The isolationist vision of models binds the notion of their epistemic value to their application and representation regarding our world. A consistent *autonomist* vision, however, maintains that it is possible to learn from models just by constructing and manipulating them, without making any reference to their capacity to refer to any extra-model reality. In several of her works, Tarja Knuuttila (2004) claims that models are constructed freely, and that valuable information is obtained from them just by constructing, examining and, particularly, manipulating them. The problem that philosophy of economics must solve however is to show how models can offer relevant and reliable knowledge about our world, and in this regard Knuuttila solution seems to be merely verbal and is based in a semantic displacement. Nobody doubts that through constructing and manipulating "objects" *something* is learned. Mathematics does it all the time in reference to some kind of abstract entity. Learning is also possible through manipulating material objects (for example, the magic cube).   But the philosophical problem that demands solution is whether the construction and manipulation of theoretical economic models allows us to learn something about *our* world, the empirical world that surrounds us, particularly about real market economies, and whether what is thus learned can somehow be used to design and to implement successful economic policies. The arguments of Knuuttila, avoid approaching these issues. In my opinion it is far more enlightening to interpret these models as the accomplishment of mere intellectual exercises. Birks, 2015, offers a similar view.

To conclude, the autonomist vision of models is perfectly consistent with theoretical practice. The failure of mainstream philosophy of economics to render account of the ability of mainstream economics to predict, explain or transform social phenomena is dodged if this perspective is adopted. It would be desirable that philosophers interested in recovering the practice of modeling in economics be committed to express it in a more explicit way, so that their merits and limitations could be appreciated with total clarity.

5. Assessing mainstream philosophy of economics

I readily concede that the analysis of models is vital for obtaining an understanding of the theoretical activity in science and also that the strategy of modeling is the usual activity of theoretical economists. It is natural then that both epistemology and philosophy of economics pay special attention to economic models. But, it does not justify (a) the pretension that embedded within theoretical models we may find some relevant and reliable knowledge about real market economies and (b) the a-critical attitude that MPE dispenses to this practice. We have just discussed point (a) at length, so let's see point (b) in more detail. Two events have had a decisive impact on the a-critical manner in which mainstream philosophical reflection about economic models is actually conducted. In the first place, traditional methodology has been undergoing a deep crisis for some decades. Under the influence of Popper and Lakatos it showed a high degree of independence with respect to current scientific activity, trying less to describe it than to critically evaluate and transform its practice. It is hard now to find followers of this tradition. Current philosophy of economics advances no proposals for improving conventional economics. The most remarkable exceptions to this rule are those of Tony Lawson and his group of critical realists, and "the Babylonian" vision of the economic method supported by Sheila Dow. It seems fair to acknowledge that Sugden also seems to question the practice of building non-credible models (those devoid of "coherence").

Secondly, a "naturalistic" approach to science claiming that there is no superior knowledge to the one provided by modern science enjoys nowadays a good amount of consensus. Therefore, philosophical reflection on science cannot legitimately impose restrictions to this practice. With the exceptions above mentioned, all the proposals of economic models that we included under the MPE label try to be consistent, in minor or greater degree, with this naturalistic view. It also explains the spread of a philosophical commitment to "recover the practice" of the economists, showing a systematic effort to exhibit the rationality of maintream's modeling practice.[5]

In principle, the "naturalistic" view of economics seems to be endorsed for reasons that are out of the question. If we label a practice as "scientific", this decision reveals that we are attributing to it a capacity to offer reliable knowledge. In the case of some venerable theoretical practices, like those of physics or biology, such consideration does not face serious opposition. But other practices do not enjoy similar respect regarding their capacities to provide qualified knowledge. What credit shall we give to a naturalistic philosophy applied to astrology or rhabdomancy?

In an intermediate situation, the scientific status of the so-called social sciences is disputable. Does the scientific approach provide political sciences with relevant and reliable knowledge about their intended

---

[5] It is worth noting that "to recover the practice" can be understood in two different ways. It can consist of exhibiting a model's rationality in the way in which the logic of the situation does (Popper, 1996), which allows one to understand the particular problem that the modeller wanted to solve (the questions, purposes and reasons that generate this particular contribution). Or something much more ambitious can be tried: to maintain that in spite of its apparently "unrealism" a model is objectively able to reach successfully basic epistemic values, like representing an aspect of the economic reality (its "intended target") or to provide the base to implement suitable economic policies. MPE's goal is to recover the practice of the whole production of mainstream economics in this second sense of the term.

phenomena? More to the point of this book, does the mainstream way of practicing economics offer such knowledge? In this first part of the book we have displayed some of the main philosophical objections that face those philosophers who take as a given that mainstream practice in economics is scientific and provides relevant contributions for the advancement of knowledge about our world. Besides, as was indicated, there are other (non-orthodox) approaches that reject these merits (and whose voices are not necessarily deprived of authority). It is questionable to take as given that mainstream modeling is an empirical science. It would be welcome if sympathetic philosophers argued this point more at length. And more than arguments, it is necessary to show *what practical results* come about from that practice. If results of this kind were provided nobody would dare to dismiss its status as a legitimate empirical discipline.

On the other hand, even if mainstream modeling is not an empirical science, it is certainly useful to *recover* this practice. The vision that better attains this goal is the *autonomist* branch of MPE. In fact, current theoretical practices in economics fit very well the type of activity that Kuhn designated as "normal science". It aims at the construction of models in order to solve well defined and precise problems, strictly technical endeavors, most of them based on previous models built within the framework of a preexisting theory (paradigm). Not surprisingly then this practice often reflects just the interests of the scientific community and are not necessarily relevant regarding immediate human necessities.

This practice leads to results that are disconnected from what most people (and also other social scientists and extra-communitarian economists) consider urgent and important economic problems[6]. It is understandable then the perplexity that it produces in people who do not belong to the exclusive community of specialists, and the difficulty that those philosophers who get along with it find when a well-argued defense of mainstream practice which demonstrates its epistemic relevance is attempted.

---

[6] It also fuels the suspicion that theoretical economic models do not necessarily contribute to the representation of some aspects of the real world, nor to the understanding of those what society considers relevant economic problems and whose solution demands from the economists.

Are models really necessary for theoretical practice in economics?

The success of the scientific approach to economics may be assessed from an historical perspective. From the beginning of the XIX century, economists with philosophical formation (like Mill, Senior and Cairnes) have offered reason as the means to ground the superiority of the theoretical practice embodied in the *Principles* of David Ricardo. They promoted its scientific status as distinct from the knowledge of economic affairs shared by common men and entrepreneurs. Their view seems more justifiable nowadays in reference to models that exhibit great technical sophistication and deductive rigor, as it is very clear that they cannot be used nor be constructed by untrained men. But it is doubtful that they contain a knowledge superior to what is already available without them. In fact, there is a good amount of economic wisdom that can be expressed in a verbal way, which preexists and is available without the contribution of any kind of theoretical modeling. Leaving aside Rosenberg's extreme positions about the necessity that one discipline must deliver successful predictions to deserve the label of science, his message that no novel or surprising results have been discovered by means of the modern practice of theoretical modeling deserves to be taken seriously (Rosenberg, 1992). The MPE tacitly recognizes this point. It does it in an indirect and shamefaced way, enhancing the role that "stories" or the "narrative" have for a correct interpretation of the (otherwise hard to grasp) messages of theoretical models (Morgan, 2012). In a similar way Cartwright interprets models as parables, and Colander and Sugden maintain that to capture the meaning and content of theoretical models additional skills and background knowledge are needed. All of them agree that there is valuable information contained in theoretical models, but do not manage to provide a clear description of it and are unable to point out what this particular contribution exactly is.

To my view, in so doing they admit that independently of the formalism and the technical unfolding, the main content of models can be expressed in those few lines incorporated in the story and written up in simple and plain language. So then, why be so committed to building models? Because it is usually evident that those "stories" that specify what the model wants to affirm or contains as a message allude to rather familiar phenomena. In fact, as I tried to make clear in chapter 2, models are usually constructed to show something that was already well known beforehand!

6. Concluding remarks

In this first part of the book the philosophical reasons offered by MPE to legitimize mainstream economic models are criticized. Not only have I maintained that its empirical and practical relevance have not been argued, but also suggested that if the sort of "knowledge" that supposedly has to be provided consists of invariant regularities (that is, laws or mechanisms), few hopes of success can be expected. If, as we have characterized them in the second part of this work, the economic processes are open ended, intervenible, based on expectations and pervaded by unavoidable conflicting interests, I do not see how theoretical models could provide significantly better knowledge than what is offered by practical knowledge and common sense.

Part II

Mechanisms, uncertainty and economic processes

Rethinking theoretical economics and philosophy of economics

Chapter 4
New mechanistic approach. Spontaneous and designed economic mechanisms

Introduction

The methodology of the first half of the 20th century installed the idea that nature and society were commanded by universal laws and that the task of sciences (natural and social) were to discover them and use this knowledge for predicting and explaining. The concept of "law" occupied the center of the scene in such concepts as logical empiricism (Hempel, Nagel) and falsificationism (Popper), as well as in some more sophisticated approaches inspired in the previous ones (Lakatos). The existence of such laws of universal validity was questioned later (Cartwright, 1983) and recently numerous authors have proposed they should be replaced by the concept of "mechanism" (Bechtel and Abrahamsen, 2005; Glennan, 1996; MDC, 2000; Glennan, 2008).

The new mechanistic literature postulates the existence of mechanisms operating in reality that generate the phenomena we observe, and maintains that the task of science (especially of natural sciences) is to discover them (Bechtel and Abrahansen, 2005). Hedstrom and Swedbeg (1998a) have maintained a similar position regarding society and the social sciences. Their vision agrees with the usual way in which economists express themselves, frequently referring to economic mechanisms. It is worth then exploring whether this perspective is helpful for a better understanding of theoretical practice in economics.

A mechanism is a sequence of entities or events connected to each other in a stable way and that, once triggered, yields an observable result .The invariant sequence has three distinguishing characteristics: a) constant parts; b) constant relations between the parts; c) if isolated the sequence works uninterruptedly, once shot.

At the level of the representations it is possible to describe different types of social and economic mechanisms. That is to say, mechanisms that if they were to act in a certain situation X would generate (and for that reason would explain) a certain behavior Y at the individual or collective level. Some of these mechanisms are merely *possible* (in the logical sense of the term, which includes purely imaginary mechanisms). Other mechanisms are more realistic, in the sense that given what we know about individuals and the institutions in which they act, it seems very probable (although it is not certain that this is the case) they can be operative in the generation of the events in which we are interested. We designate them as *feasible* mechanisms.

In this chapter I examine a spontaneous mechanism of decision making with the sole purpose of laying out the foundations to describe other mechanisms, more interesting for us, that are the product of deliberate design (in Mechanism Design and Libertarian Paternalism). These different types of designed mechanisms are compared to each other and some of the conditions that allow that invariant sequences of socially desirable events may be implemented are analyzed. Thus we hope to show how relatively exceptional are these conditions, opening the door for examining the appropriate approach in those domains where these conditions do not appear: i.e., in reference to open-ended economic processes – internally conflictive and intervenibles – based on expectations, which is the central concept of this book.

1. Spontaneous mechanisms

1.1. Belief Formation Mechanisms (BFM)

Economists are interested in finding out the way expectations are formed. There have been several attempts to model this formation as a mechanism (see Gordon, 1978, pp. 182-183). The central controversy has focused on whether it is or not an adaptive mechanism. One of the more used mechanisms incorporates the Bayesian approach for the updating of beliefs. Another case is the mechanism of election between lotteries described in Expected Utility Theory. All the cases are variants of what Hausman (1992) has called "intentional mechanisms".

How realistic are they? It seems that most of them are rather *possible* mechanisms (rational ex-post reconstructions whose aim is to identify conditions that providing they occur some interesting results will ensue). Those who propose these mechanisms are not interested in determining if they are *really* responsible for the way in which agents come to hold their beliefs. Their intent is just to point out that if their action in market economies is assumed, some observed results will be compatible with them.

A well-known mechanism consisting of regular interactions between people is what Granovetter called "belief formation mechanism" (see Hedström and Swedberg, 1998a). The basic idea is that the behavior of other people sends a signal that is received and generates a functional relation that could be causally interpreted. For example, the growing patronizing of a restaurant induces other individuals to go themselves. A mechanism of this type can be formalized this way:

$$b_{it}a = f(n_{t-1}, a)$$

which means that the belief *b* of an individual *i* in time *t* about the convenience of performing an action *a* is a (growing) function of the number of individuals that have performed *a* before.

It is certainly successful as long as it is considered just a *possible* mechanism. Many phenomena are compatible with this representation that tries to model a certain form of imitative behavior. Thus we can explain for example, why people do not enter empty restaurants and instead crowd together standing in line in full restaurants. Of course, flocking behavior can be explained this way.

But for them to be explanatory mechanisms, they also have to be *feasible*, and there some problems arise. Some of them are suggested by the following questions. How general is this mechanism? How much of its explanatory value is dependent of its particular characteristics and the way the situation is described? Can it be said that any individual increases his belief that he must look for work if others do it? Would you enter a popular venue because it is much attended? Will you stand in line in front of a shop just because others are doing so?

Two points deserve to be stressed here: (a) Not all the signals we receive invite imitation. If many people begin to move to district X, some that already live there because it is relatively quiet and isolated will have an incentive to move out; and others that initially were planning to move to X looking for tranquility and low population density, will reconsider; (b) Other people's behavior sends divergent signals, that are interpreted by the individuals in light of their beliefs and preferences (i.e. they can be diversely interpreted).

The imitative mechanism works when it is assumed that the referred class of individuals is relatively homogenous. For example, companions at table who recognize themselves as sharing identical tastes. A person A that is sitting at a dinner table may be influenced by the behavior of others at the same table, B, C, etc., because she considers (she believes) that her gastronomical preferences are represented by those of B, C, etc. Homogeneity is required to deactivate subjectivism.

The imitative mechanism is relevant in post-Keynesian tradition. On the one hand the importance of aping behavior goes back to Keynes (1937), where it is said that under conditions of uncertainty imitation is one of the "techniques" to which individuals resort to take decisions. Nevertheless, as stated in the following chapter, contrary to Keynes' view this technique does not seem to be a good strategy for contexts where true uncertainty predominates (but it is certainly a clever response for those conditions in which complexity reigns).

On the other hand imitative behavior between peers has been introduced in the post-Keynesian theory of consumer demand. Here the idea is that the fact that somebody belongs to a social group induces him to consume what is characteristic of that group. When changing social standing, people change their reference group (and accordingly, a change in their habits of consumption fitting the new situation is verified). In my view the post-

Keynesian theory of consumer behavior better illustrates a system of preference-formation than one of belief-formation.

Anyway, it is more accurate to say that given uncertainty the individual consumption behavior depends on the pattern of consumption of one's reference group. It does not have so much to do with the number of people as with status. The post-Keynesian consumer does not enter a restaurant because there are many patrons, but because these customers are his peers. He wishes to exhibit a behavior of consumption fitting his social position.

1.2 Transmission mechanisms (macroeconomics)

Economics usually refers to transmission mechanisms. They are often *macro*economic mechanisms, in which certain changes in a set of economic variables produce modifications in another set of economic variables. Let us see some examples of how they work and some of the problems that this strategy shows (what follows is based on Snowdon and Vane, 1997). These mechanisms operate in the intermediate portion of the AS curve:

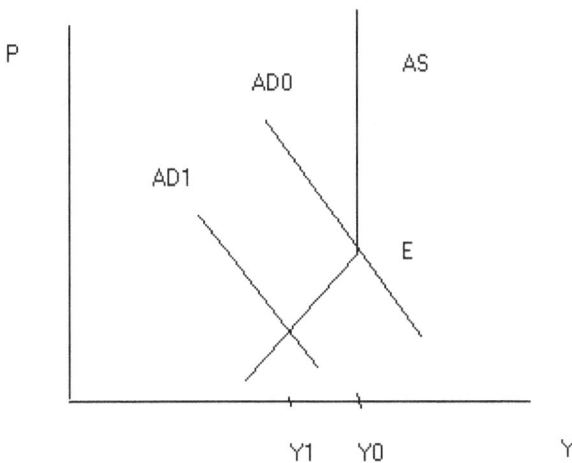

As usual, P stands for prices, Y for income (production), AD for aggregated demand and AS for aggregated supply. It is also assumed that P is flexible, but W is downright rigid. In these conditions, involuntary unemployment can emerge (i.e., equilibrium with unemployment). The sequence is the following:

1) The starting point is an equilibrium situation with full employment and income Y0.
2) AD drops causing that income and employment to diminish to Y1. As the reduction of demand makes prices drop and W remains fixed, the real wage increases causing a reduction in production and employment.
3) The economy may stagnate around Y1. This is called a state of "balance" (Boland introduces this terminology to distinguish this situation from that of equilibrium with full employment)

From this situation different models are developed in order to explore what circumstances (mechanisms) would push the economy again to a situation of full employment (and what circumstances could prevent this). Only some of these mechanisms contemplate the intervention of the State.

a. Interventionist model

Within the framework of the orthodox Keynesian approach (i.e., a macroeconomic view based on Keynes, minus radical uncertainty and "animal spirits"), some economists explore whether the increase of Government expenses can redirect (by increasing AD) the economy to full employment. What is modeled is a *possible* mechanism able to generate this result. Here "possible" does not have only a logical sense; it sets out a mechanism that describes a plausible economic path: a sequence of economic events whose accomplishment is *feasible* (compatible with all we know about human behavior under these sorts of economic restrictions).

It is assumed that if the state increases its expenses a deficit arises that must be covered by means of taxes or by issuing bonds. If the former is dismissed because it would produce "crowding out", what remains is to issue bonds. The problem that this model tries to solve is by what means/mechanism the practice of issuing bonds would reset the economy back to full employment. The proposed solution is based on the so called wealth-effect. The frame is provided by an IS–LM model, and the usual sequence follows these steps.

a) Bonds make the private sector richer;
b) As wealth augments, consumption increases and Md grows;
c) Both results have opposed effects respect to the aggregated income (Y). The increase of consumption moves IS to the right, and the increase of Md moves LM to the left.
d) If the wealth effect prevails it amounts to greater consumption, the government deficit will disappear and the added production and employment will increase.

An obvious question is how do we know that the "wealth-effect" will be generated? The doubts regarding the feasibility that this may indeed happen are summarized in the so-called "Ricardian debt equivalence". The private sector (that acquires bonds) contracts future obligations (payment of interest). If it takes full account of these obligations, it will not consider bonds as net wealth. Therefore, instead of increasing consumption, agents will save more to pay their debts. A usual rebuttal to this objection is that the private sector does not make such calculations. Evidently, whether the model is able to solve or not its intended problem depends on how the rationality and the expectations of the agents is modeled. The feasibility of the proposed mechanism can then be defended arguing the "unrealism" of the conditions that would prevent their operation. But even if the entrepreneurs considered bonds as wealth, a new question arises about how we can know that the wealth-effect will prevail. Positing that this will be the case is advisable because without it the balance will not be recovered. But it may not ensue at all.

The answer to both questions is that at heart "we do not know". They are not questions that can be answered ex-ante, by empirical means or introspection. The way in which the agents react can vary from a moment to the next and may be different in different societies. Nevertheless, the existence of the wealth-effect and its predominance is the key of the mechanism of adjustment. This shows that although it is a feasible mechanism (not merely possible in the logical sense of the term), the sequence may never attain the desired results. As it will be argued, to guarantee its success additional practical measures will have to be taken.

b. Adjusting models without intervention

b. 1. Neoclassical synthesis (NS)

It asserts that the free operation of the price system returns the economy to full employment, with no need of governmental intervention. To reach this result the assumption that W is flexible is incorporated. This idea cannot be found in Keynes, but is assumed by classic and neoclassic economists, who claimed that wage reductions would increase the employment level. The transmission mechanism is like this:

In Y1 the prevailing real wage is too high and there is excess of supply in the work market. The competition between workers causes W to drop dragging prices with it, because W is one of the central components of the costs. For that reason, P drops in greater measure that it would have done had W remained rigid. The real value of M is then increased. The excess of money is channeled to the bonds market whose prices goes up and causes a drop in the interest rates. A fall in interest rates stimulates investment and AD therefore increases, moderating the drop of P. Assuming that W falls more quickly than P, real wages decrease until full employment is reached. The complete sequence is as follows:

$$\downarrow W \rightarrow \downarrow P \rightarrow +\Delta M \rightarrow +\Delta \text{ Bonds Demand} \rightarrow -\Delta i \rightarrow +\Delta I \rightarrow +\Delta (Y, L)$$
$$(1) \hspace{5cm} (2)$$

Schema 1

The economy goes from an initial equilibrium with unemployment to a new equilibrium with full employment, with no need of state intervention. What NS proposes is a noninterventionist mechanism, via free prices and the unregulated operation of the labor market.

The procedure deserves some commentaries. In the first place, the fact that both models (interventionist and NS) are feasible regarding the behavior of W, although they have opposite positions, shows that this behavior is not commanded by the workings of natural laws (or social-natural laws). Like all economic phenomena, W's behavior depends on an institutional context and on changing (and potentially manipulable) expectations. Among other things, it depends on the level and the attitude of union organizations. Different institutional scenarios could have different impact on W's flexibility.

Secondly, NS proposes an adjustment via prices and operation of the labor market. Particularly, NS takes the real wage as an explanatory variable of the changes in employment, which is not consistent with Keynes' view in his General Theory (chapter 2) that there is no such market. In GT both employment and production are unilaterally determined by the firms' decisions. Is there or not a labor market? Do workers' decisions influence employment and production levels or not? As in the case of the flexibility of W, both positions are opposite but feasible.

Evidently, whichever way these questions can be answered the referred phenomena are not subject to immutable laws of nature known ex-ante (of the sort of "workers do not influence employment decisions"). They depend instead on circumstances that must be found out empirically ex-post, and on the correlation of forces between workers and firms. The relations between workers and entrepreneurs can be different from one time to another and from a region to another; in addition, it can be modified by different sorts of deliberate intervention, that range from coercion to negotiation. In different institutional arrangements workers and firms can enjoy diverse degrees of influence. And it is possible to take measures to implement those adjustments that are more advisable. In fact, in Argentina this kind of negotiation is regularly made by means of the so called "*paritarias*", which are negotiations between firms and unions designed to find an agreement on the level of wages.

Although no one doubts that NS involves a *possible* mechanism, it could be *not feasible*, or at least not easily attainable, due to the reasons that are mentioned next. The conventional vision embodied in NS concedes the whole protagonist role to the firms. They are who, taking into account the drop in real wages, increase investments, causing AD to move in the direction of full employment. The increase in I is translated as an increase in AD (not in the displacement of AS). Granting some power to the workers and imagining different institutional adjustments the sequence may have different outcomes.

b. 2. Obstacles to the NS's mechanism

There are other reasons, more strictly economic, to question the automatism of the described self-adjustment gear. Even if W is flexible, it is possible for the adjustment not to occur due to two circumstances: the so-called trap of liquidity and the non elasticity of investment respect to changes in the interest rate. That is to say, the operation of the mechanism postulated by the Neoclassical Synthesis, that connects ΔM with ΔY and ΔL, can be blocked due to different types of rigidities. This indicates that in the middle portion of the AS curve a self-adjusting mechanism does not exist.

Liquidity-trap

The mechanism can be interrupted at point (1) of *schema 1*. Maybe because the excess of money is not channeled to the bonds market, but used to buy speculative balances. This would prevent I from falling down enough to prompt (via investments) an increase in added demand which will be sufficient to moderate the fall of P. When this causal chain is blocked, P falls proportionally to W (balanced deflation), the real wages do not drop and the labor market does not clear. The sequence would be this:

$\downarrow$W $\rightarrow$ $\downarrow$P $\rightarrow$ $+\Delta$M $\rightarrow$ $+\Delta$ Demand of speculative balances $\rightarrow$ i "sticky" $\rightarrow$ Balanced Deflation $\rightarrow$ Unemployment persistence

Schema 2

Again, there are no doubts about the feasibility of such a mechanism. Clearly it is not an arbitrary or capricious sequence. It is worth then to ask what causes the excess of money to be channeled to the bond market and not to speculative balances? Is it not the case that central to achieving this result is the set of institutional and legal arrangements that prevail, the creation of novel economic instruments that make bonds more attractive, as well as the sort of political agreements that are reached? The relevant theoretical task is not to discover the authentic "law" that leads from a change in a set of variables to well defined changes in other group of variables, but to examine the conditions under which different feasible sequences are realized (as well as the diverse ways to modify those conditions and those results). On these bases, practically oriented economists can work to obtain desired results. In fact, all the relevant actors (including the government) take part all along the sequence by pushing in the way that they expect will favor their interests.

Inelastic investment regarding the interest rate

This is a second objection to NS. In this case the initial mechanism is interrupted at (2) in *Schema 1*. Although the interest rate drops (possibly because part of the excess of M went to the bonds market) it does not decline sufficiently. For that reason, I and AD increase but not enough to lead the economy back at the level of full employment. What would a "sufficient" reduction be? It is not obvious. But assuming that we are able to quantify it, investments also seem to be sensitive to other questions that have nothing to do with the level of the interest rate. In the last instance, as Keynes indicated, everything depends on the expectations that agents form, and in turn they depend on a multitude of influences that we will examine in the following chapter.

b. 3. Pigou's Effect

The English economist Arthur Pigou proposed a mechanism showing that the two mentioned rigidities (liquidity trap and inelasticity of investment respect to the interest rate) are not decisive: if W is flexible, the economy can return at the equilibrium level with full employment.

Mechanism: $\downarrow P \rightarrow +\Delta M \rightarrow +\Delta$ Consumption $\rightarrow +\Delta (Y, L)$

Schema 3

His central argument is that an increase in the real value of money can move both curves, LM and IS towards the right and the balance can be recovered. He shows that the original equilibrium with unemployment depends on the crucial assumption that W remains rigid. If it is assumed, instead, that W is flexible, nothing in principle would prevent the economy from reaching equilibrium with full employment (not even the two additional rigidities pointed out by Keynes, which made him distrust the effectiveness of monetary policies).

Possibility, feasibility and attainability

Although no doubt exists that the examined mechanisms are possible, and in most cases are feasible, it may happen that they could not be *attainable*. These mechanisms are sequences of events, which can prevail or not, according to how are agents' expectations, the characteristics of the institutions in which their decisions are framed and the influence that the actions of very diverse groups of economic action (corporations, unions, political parties, mass media, journalists, etc.) have on them. Both expectations and institutions are modifiable, and can be influenced by groups of interests and individuals with lobbying capacity. Therefore they are not spontaneous clockwork mechanisms. They are alternative sequences, all of them feasible that depend on external assistance for their fulfillment.

Granting that they are feasible sequences, their implementation can be difficult or impossible, because none of the partners is strong enough to generate the expectations that are required and to impose the set of institutions that are needed. Therefore, the sequence that ultimately prevails does not express a kind of natural order: it has been socially constituted, and it may well not have happened. History is full of attempts to naturalize the prevailing social relations. Today it is clear that presumed natural laws, like the incapacity of women to assume government responsibilities, were just social constructions. We will return to these points later.

2. Designed mechanisms

Three kinds of mechanisms artificially designed to generate desired results are examined: Prospect Theory – Libertarian Paternalism (PT – PL); Mechanism Design (MD) and Research Assessment System (RAS).

2.1 Libertarian Paternalism (LP)

Economists may build two different sorts of models: those that represent the markets and those that represent individual decisions whose results enter the market mechanisms as input. We call this last kind of models Decision Making Models (in short, DMM)[1]. Simon (1986) has distinguished between substantive and procedural DMM. Substantive models are only interested in the results of individual decisions (for instance, assuming risk or uncertainty, which of a set of lotteries will be picked up by an individual with well-defined preferences and expectations). Instead, Procedural models depict the processes of decision making, i.e. the way in which people choose among alternative prospects. There are two different kinds of procedural models. Simon's Procedural models were intended to represent the way in which people actually perform the calculations that result in their particular choices. Simon thought that real people could not maximize but were able to do far more simple calculations designed to satisfy their expectations. In his view people have goals, face alternative means to reach them, and evaluate which of these means will be appropriate for reaching their goals in a satisfactory way (Simon, 1955). Usually people do good enough calculations and this is why these representation models were called models of Procedural Rationality. This is a rather "illuminist" view of the individual process of decision making. Prospect Theory (Kahneman and Tversky, 1979) and many Behavioral Economic models are a different sort of procedural models. They represent individual decisions as psychologically (rather than rationally) driven. For instance, individuals whose preferences are represented as reflecting loss aversion (Thaler, 1980; Kahneman, Knetsch and Thaler, 1991; Tversky and Kahneman, 1992) or taking decisions founded on mental accounts (Thaler, 1985), are not making any kind of calculation when deciding. They are rather reacting in a non-deliberate manner to the information received. Behavioral models that incorporate psychological resources to represent the way in which individuals make decisions under risk or uncertainty may be called Behavioral Procedural Models (BPM). They provide a causal explanation of anomalous economic patterns that allows for extra market intervention and manipulability in order to correct and improve some key individual decisions.

---

[1] Some part of the content of section 2.1. has been published in the *Journal of Philosophical Economics*, volume V, issue 2 (spring 2012).

This capacity sets the basis for the so called libertarian paternalism (Sunstein and Thaler, 2003).

The contribution of Cognitive Psychology to the way in which decisions are made

Cognitive Psychology claims that in making decisions people may use two different cognitive systems (Kahneman, 2003): an intuitive system (S1) and a more rational system (S2). Experimental research shows that S2 exercises an effective control on S1 only under some special circumstances. In most cases in which people have to make choices under real circumstances, they use elements of their intuitive system, which may be classified as propensities (for instance, "loss aversion", "overconfidence" and "mental accounts") and heuristics (like, "default rule", "fifty-fifty", "representativeness"). Loss aversion is the most appreciated theoretical resource among behavioral economists and it is used in a majority of models (for illustrations of this use, see Camerer and Loewenstein, 2004 and Ho et. Al, 2006). The so called Asian Disease is a paradigmatic example of the way in which loss aversion may alter individual decisions (Kahneman, 2003, pp. 1458.). To illustrate, imagine that the United States is preparing for the outbreak of an unusual Asian disease, which is expected to kill 600 people. Two alternative programs to combat the disease have been proposed. Assume also that the exact scientific estimates of the consequences of the programs are as follows:

If Program A is adopted, 200 people will be saved.
If Program B is adopted, there is a one-third probability that 600 people will be saved and a two-thirds probability that no people will be saved.

Suppose now that a group of individuals is asked to choose one of these options. Experimental results show that most individuals choose Program A over Program B, revealing risk aversion. In a next round they are asked to pick up among these two transformed options:

If Program A' is adopted, 400 people will die.
If Program B' is adopted, there is a one third probability that nobody will die and a two-thirds probability that 600 people will die.

Spontaneous and designed economic mechanisms

Now a majority of individuals choose Program B' over Program A' revealing love to risk (or, as Kahneman and Tversky said, loss aversion). A surprising result given that both pairs of options refer exactly to the same circumstances. The only difference is that the first couple of options is described in terms of gains (lives saved) and the second in terms of losses (lives lost). The way in which options are described matters for decision makers!

Several different propensities and heuristics other than loss aversion have been identified in many different experimental settings applied to economics. They identify and make explicit the particular psychological process that results in (or contributes to) a pattern invested with economic relevance. For achieving this goal the contribution of Cognitive Psychology is crucial in helping to give shape to the particular structure of BP models. Here are a few examples.

First. Benartzi and Thaler (1995) offer a specific example of a Behavioral procedural model built along these lines. The basic motivation for building this model is the existence of an anomalous pattern: the so-called Equity Premium Puzzle (EPP). The EPP is the difference between the return in stocks and the return on a risk free asset (for instance, treasury bills). In the USA, for the last 100 years equity premium has been around 7 points. It is called a puzzle because this difference is too large to be explained by standard economic models. In fact, the standard risk-aversion explanation is highly implausible. Mehra and Presscot (1985) found that in order to explain the puzzle in a traditional way, a coefficient of risk aversion should be close to 30 although the actual estimation is close to 1.

Modeling individual preferences as having loss aversion and assuming myopia as the triggering variable, Benartzi and Thaler (1995) manage to obtain the anomalous pattern.

Second. Kahneman and Thaler (1991) explore the economic consequences of compensation policy. Broadly speaking, they argue that the pattern of individual consumption and consequently the utility derived from it could be modified by changing the flow of compensation individuals receive, even if the total amount of compensation received remains constant.[2] Following the ideas of Scitovsky (1976), Kahneman and Thaler distinguish between comfort and pleasure goods. Comforts are things that people buy and then get accustomed to, not generating utility in the long run. In contrast, pleasures are things people do not adapt to, increasing their utility. They claim that people tend to spend in comfort goods what they consider their regular incomes and tend to buy pleasure goods with that part of their incomes that is considered as extra-payment. Both the number of extra-payments received and their amounts are key variables influencing the patterns of their consumption decisions.

The notion of adaptation level plays a central role in their argument. They find that in order to enhance the intensity of a particular sensation, it should be made intermittent over time, and that a single experience is less likely to modify the reference level as long as it is viewed as unusual. Sudden changes are evaluated as a distinctive departure from adaptation, whereas a very slow gradual change will drag the adaptation level along with it, and may not even be detected (Kahneman and Thaler, 1991). The implication of this analysis for economics is rather direct: to the extent that people become quickly adapted to a consumption pattern obtained by their regular level of remuneration, increases in wages will have no effect on utility in the long run. However, a flow of income that induces people to increase their expenditure in pleasure goods will not drag the adaptation level along with it. These findings suggest that in a given period people will get more wellbeing from a flow of compensation including some extra-payments (clearly differentiated from what they consider their regular salary) than what they get from receiving a single amount of money (even if the total amount of money is the same in both cases). Then it would be possible to "create more

---

[2] Furthermore, Kahneman and Thaler (1991) assert that the pattern of consumption affects the amount of utility individuals get from one fixed amount of money.
"The general conclusion is that it is certainly possible to use the same amount of money to produce different amounts of utility! The suggestion is that, for an income stream that is sufficient to prevent serious deprivation ..., there exists a positively skewed distribution of the income over time that will yield greater utility than an even distribution. In particular, taking a portion of the compensation and paying it in a lump sum would appear to make things better." (Kahneman and Thaler ,1991, pp.342-343)

worker satisfaction without increasing the cost of the pay packages" (Kahneman and Thaler, 1991, p. 341).[3]

A third example of the way in which interventions may move the reference point and change an agent's economic decisions is provided by Bernartzy and Thaler (2001), who examine how people choose among defined contribution saving plans, which combine different sorts of investments (e.g., bonds and equities). They provide evidence that individuals "make decisions that seem to be based on naive (or confused) notions of diversifications" (p.79), which may not be optimal. One such heuristic is the so-called 1/n strategy, which means that individuals "divide their contributions evenly across the funds offered in the plan" (Bernartzy and Thaler, 2001, p.79). They find that "the array of funds offered to plan participants can have a surprisingly strong influence on the assets they end up owning" (p. 96). Therefore, the way in which the options are presented to the decision-makers seems to matter. As a result, as long as standard economic theory provides a benchmark for identifying the best option, an opportunity for helping people by framing their decisions in the "correct" way is created.

Some considerations about LP's technologies

Libertarian Paternalism is an economic technology that influences peoples' decisions by imposing the reference point according to what individuals rank as their preferences among alternative lotteries. It is a *paternalistic* technology because individuals are induced to choose an alternative that has been picked up for them by other persons (the "observers") that impose the frame. But it is *libertarian* because decision makers make the choice by themselves: individuals are induced to pick up just one of the alternatives but not forced to do it. It is also an *altruistic* technology because the induced option is presumed to be the one that is best for him. Agents are saved from themselves, so to speak: if their actual decisions were not influenced they would regret their results in the future.

A key feature of all the forms of paternalism considered is that "observers" do not pretend to know some sort of economic "laws" or "mechanisms" that

---

[3] This section largely follows the arguments developed in a co-authored paper (see Ivarola et al., *Economic Thought*, Vol. 2, N° 2, October 2013.

are beyond the consideration of plain individuals. What they know better is a wide set of psychological biases that influence the agents' behavior and their typical reactions when the information received has certain structural features. The observers have access to a theory (Prospect Theory) that correlates changes in the point of reference of the decision set with changes in decisions.

It is interesting that even if libertarian paternalism defies conventional theories of decision making it uses and takes for granted a good part of standard economics. As Bernartzy and Thaler (2001, p. 79) have shown in many cases paternalistic interventions aims at helping people to approach those results that have been identified as optimal by standard economics. In this sense conventional economics plays a key role in libertarian paternalism providing the benchmark that has to be reached or approximate.

Although libertarian paternalism has been applied within economics, its technologies may be extended to some other interesting domains (as the choice among political parties, for instance). A severe limitation of this technology however is that the kind of problems to which it applies is very restricted focusing on individual decisions among lotteries. Regarding more ample scenarios characterized by fundamental uncertainty and the coexistence of conflicting interests its usefulness is unclear. Most traditional economical problems belong to this latter domain. For them, other kinds of technologies, if possible at all, are needed.

2.2. Mechanism Design (MD)

The kernel of Mechanism Design (MD) is "matching', what "is the part of economics that focuses on the question of who gets what, particularly when the scarce goods to be allocated are heterogeneous and indivisible; for example, who works at which job, which students go to which school, who receives which transplantable organ, and so on" (Muriel Niederle, Alvin E. Roth and Tayfun Sönmez, 2007).

These problems are solved by building "mechanisms" (algorithms or institutional designs) which rely on basic tools of game theory in order to match rankings of preferences. There are many successful designs of this kind. One of them is "the design of auctions through which the U.S. Federal Communications Commission sells the rights to transmit on different parts of the radio spectrum" (Alexandrova, 2006; Alexandrova and Northcott, 2008b). Another particularly successful case of matching is "the design of labor clearinghouses such as the one through which American doctors get their first jobs" (Roth, 2002; 2010).

> "Nowadays, a medical student applies to hospitals and goes on interviews in the winter of the final year of medical school, and then in February submits an ordered preference list of positions to the centralized clearing house, the National Resident Matching Program (NRMP). At the same time, the residency programs (the employers) submit an ordered preference list of candidates. Once all the preference lists are collected, the clearing house uses an algorithm to produce a match, and residency programs and applicants are informed to whom they have been matched" (Niederle et. al., 2007).

A strong anti-interventionist tradition exists in economics which assumes that markets regularly work well without any regulation. According to this view any of the following two conditions should be met for intervention to be admissible (Maskin, 2008):

a) Lack of market power: "there are large numbers of buyers and sellers, so that no single agent has significant market power";

b) Lack of externalities: "there are no significant externalities, that is, an agent's consumption, production, and information does not affect others' production or consumption".

According to Maskin "mechanisms improving the market are generally possible if either assumption is violated" (Maskin, 2008). In such case it is possible to design a mechanism that outperforms the autonomous working of the markets. These remarks open the door for some interesting problems:

1) Whether MD is or not a feasible strategy should be decided on an empirical basis and case by case, looking at the structure of the

particular market under consideration. In line with the views of authors like Lawson and Dow ontological considerations have priority in order to decide whether the tools of game theory are applicable for improving the workings of a given market;

2) How much of the whole economy may be bettered implementing some form of mechanism of the type that MD generates is not clear. The situation is similar to that described in the case of libertarian paternalism. In fact, the domain of application of techniques like that of MD seems to be extremely narrow. If there is an extended domain of imperfect markets commanded by mega-firms, as some post-Keynesians assert (see Arestis, 1992) there is ample room for helpful interventions, but surely not of the kinds that MD provides.

3) An interesting point is whether the successful application of algorithms could be extended to more traditional economic domains, like public goods, financial markets or economic development. My impression is that in such cases the kind of knowledge that game theory provides is not as central as it is to gather enough political power to enforce the required institutions. Traditional philosophy of economics presumes that the solution of every economic problem rests in finding more and better scientific knowledge. MD's advocates are not the exception, even if they allow for an interdisciplinary team of scientific workers:

> "the (ir) design of the entry level labor market for American doctors ..... was able to profitably employ theory, historical observation, experimentation, and computation" (Roth, 2002).

Regarding economics problems in which redistribution (of income or wealth) or growth is the central point, may anyone think that the solution depends on finding technological means (as it is, for instance, a particular design of an application form or a sophisticated software) apt to induce the parts to elicit their true preferences? Or does anyone think that, in case the elicitation problem could be successfully solved, there is a scientific solution (an algorithm) for matching opposite preferences? It seems more reasonable to imagine that in those cases intervention must consist of a wide set of regulations and institutions whose characteristics are unknowable beforehand, and in any case they should be enforced against the will of those economic agents that are deprived of some privileges. In most transcendental economic problems the difficulty for solving them is not poor information or absence of scientific knowledge. What is lacking is the amount of power needed for setting off transformations that affect powerful economic groups. The difficulty is not scientific, but political.[4]

Finally, in the case of the allocation of public goods individual preferences could be less relevant than other strategic goals that the government could be aiming at. What kind of energy people prefer taking into account ecological considerations and security is something of concern for governments. But what types of energy are more convenient in terms of costs, regional development, national security and integration with other regions and countries could be equally important. Take for instance the implementation of a retirement system. Even if it is possible that most people would prefer to keep (and administer by themselves) their whole wage (a conduct in line with the Austrian's "preference by time"), the government may note that in this particular case attending individual preferences would be pernicious for individual themselves in the long run, deciding to go ahead with this sort of paternalistic system.

2.3 Mechanisms that cumulate power: RAS

RAS is an institution designed to evaluate the quality of the different branches of scientific investigation en Great Britain. It is examined by Gillies (2013) and even if it is not an economic mechanism it is interesting to take it into account as a reference point in order to illuminate some aspects of PL and MD which have not been mentioned until now. Mechanisms similar to RAS are implemented in many countries. Basically the system consists of two groups of individuals: the evaluation committee (EC) and the individual researchers (IR). The EC strongly influences the decisions of the

---

[4] On this subject, it is significant that although his article refers to the design of mechanisms of allocation of public goods, Maskin does not give a single relevant example of mechanisms of this type. He only develops this idea using a 2x2 case, written up just for illustrative effect. Their explorations (of the type of monotonicity theorems) seem to solve exclusively theoretical problems of artificial games. This is an indication of the difficulty for extending MD to relevant cases that involve allocation of public goods.

researchers through the imposition of a set of criteria in order to rank the specialized journals, set the main topics of research and consider the academic impact of their contributions.[5]

Of course researchers are free to comply or not with these rules, but their decisions have consequences in terms of employment (positions), wages and academic prestige. Many decisions taken by academic institutions (like what line of research deserves priority, or what subjects should be included or excluded within their curricula, and which scholars will be in charge) are also influenced by the same mechanism. This is so because institutions themselves are evaluated on similar bases. The quality of their academic scholars is a key component of the quality of academic institutions.

The evaluation committee may be a quite heterogeneous group, including people belonging to different traditions of research, which may have different views about the standards that should be met. But as long as one tradition is in position to impose the criteria to the remaining, RAS becomes a building-power mechanism that reinforces the original dominant position. Their results are predictable and pluralism is progressively eliminated.

3. Affinities and differences among deliberately designed mechanisms

Unlike the mechanism that we have examined at the beginning of this chapter (BFM), the designed mechanisms are *feasible* (not merely possible) mechanisms, whose operation can be stated by means of experiment or inspection. On the other hand, the imitation of other people, that is decisive in BFM, plays a secondary or null role in them. In RAS, for example, although imitative conduct between peers is verified, this takes place as a sub-product of the workings of the mechanism, which induces the researchers to adopt certain criteria. It is a mechanism in which prime calculation does not mimic what the colleagues do. It may be so because the

---

[5] RAS sets out to form researchers' preferences about what line of investigation to take or to which Journals submit their papers. It does its job by influencing researchers' expectations providing information of the results (monetary, academic and institutional) they will obtain in case they decide to comply or not with RAS' criteria.

results of the alternative decisions are known beforehand. If the so called herd effect takes place it is due to unbalanced incentives (a certain type of theoretical practice is encouraged and the alternatives lose heart).

In all of the three deliberate mechanisms we have examined the "observers" form a homogenous group regarding their interests. In PT-PL the observers share their goals and behave in a collaborative way (the group of experts impose by consensus a frame to the decision makers). Something similar happens with the mechanisms displayed by MD. The designers are regularly an interdisciplinary group cooperating for obtaining a result wanted by all. In RAS, although in the Evaluative Committee different groups with opposed interests can coexist, the majority group imposes their criteria to the other groups (as well as to the investigators).

On the other hand, a certain asymmetry of power or knowledge between observers (designers) and decision makers (agents and investigators) is verified in all these cases. In PL and RAS, as long as the designers have the capacity to settle down appropriate conditions, the choices of a majority of individuals can be commanded. These mechanisms assure designers' control of individual decisions and their predictability. The designers set the "frame" (the point of reference) deliberately influencing the decisions a majority of individuals will adopt within this frame. MD is an obvious case of asymmetry of knowledge, in which the mechanism is constructed by means of a group of experts endowed with especial skills. Nevertheless, agents' preferences impose conditions that the algorithm must satisfy. It is a technology in which the sovereignty of the "consumer" is granted. The experts have gnoseological advantage over plain individuals, but the individual's preferences must be honored. A particularity that distinguishes RAS from the other deliberate mechanisms, is that it allows an initially dominant group to be in position to reinforce its preeminence at each round of application of the criteria. It is a mechanism that allows to conserve and to increase the power of the initially dominant group.

These mechanisms show also some differences in relation to the amount of freedom enjoyed by the decision makers. RAS is the least libertarian mechanism of all of them, since although the individuals themselves are those who ultimately choose their lines of research, they are explicitly compelled to act in a well-defined way, fixed by the dominant criteria. On the other hand, their decisions are rational, in the usual sense of the term (they come about from a calculation of costs and benefits). RAS appeals to reason, not to emotions (as it seems to be the case of PL). MD is very different in this sense, since it simply takes into consideration the elicited preferences of the several players and designs an institutional mechanism able to fit them. There is neither coercion nor paternalism in this case.

Designing mechanisms is in principle in our hands and their results are neither unexpected nor inevitable. Undesired results can be eliminated by modifying the mechanism. These types of mechanisms are so frequent that their existence does not trigger philosophical perplexity.

> "Why do people abide by rules (think of traffic rules, for example)? Because they know that if they transgress the rules there is a chance they will be caught in the act... and will be punished. Why is there a system of punishing transgressors in the first place? Well, because some (particularly, ... authorities) thought it is a good idea to install such a system. This way of explaining social, aggregate behavior in terms of the intentions and the expectations of the people producing the behavior seems to make perfectly good sense... But it also has a trivial ring over it. If this type of explanation were the only type available to (and actually practiced by) social scientists, then this would make them vulnerable to the oft-cited charge that social sciences are not able to go beyond mere common sense (or 'folk') understanding. But, happily, there is a venerable tradition in social theorizing in which another, non-trivial type of explanation of social, aggregate behavior is put forward: the invisible-hand explanation" (Jaansen and Vromen, Foreward to Aydinonat, 2005).

Will the authors of the prologue be ready to dismiss the algorithms of MD? Maybe they will. Because, on the one hand they seem to think that authentic science has to do with transcendental entities, and on the other hand, a revered tradition of thought exists that has no confidence in deliberate human intervention and distrusts its beneficial effects. The crude intellectualism (i.e., a purely contemplative attitude) involved in this position makes the authors believe that to pay attention to institutions that are working fairly well at the empirical level is a marginal philosophical task. This can explain why, with a few exceptions (Alexandrova and, apparently, lately Reiss), mainstream philosophy of economics has shown little liking for MD. It is important to note, however, that the crucial task is not merely to describe these mechanisms, but to construct them and to make them work so that they may contribute to obtaining the desired goals. This eminently practical task is neither valued nor conceptualized by MPE.

In sum, PL and MD are successful technological applications of theoretical practice in economics, but their domain is limited and restricted to a few relatively exceptional scenarios, in which the agents and the designers face conditions of certainty or risk, and no significant conflicts of interest exist between the actors. In the next chapter we are going to examine one of the conditions that make these technologies inapplicable in broader scenarios, where people commonly hope that the economic theory will be able to contribute to the construction of technological solutions to the sort of sensitive problems present there.

Rethinking theoretical economics and philosophy of economics

Chapter 5
Economic processes

1. Introduction

Some authors think that economics has been successful in discovering invisible hand mechanisms. An idea closely associated to this position is to assign to social sciences and the economy the task of examining the unwanted and not deliberately pursued consequences of our present decisions (Popper, Hayek). Nevertheless, some mechanisms like PT-PL, RAS and MD that we discussed in Chapter Four, are mechanisms of *visible* hand, in which wished results are deliberately attempted (and often successfully achieved). This is possible because they are implemented in a context where certainty or risk prevails. The economic processes that we will examine next are very different: they are affected by radical *un*certainty and they cannot be analyzed on the base of theoretical models that assume some kinds of invariants of legal or mechanical type. They are better understood when approached as open-ended, conflicting and intervenible processes. For that reason they cannot be the subject of scientific knowledge, as it is usually characterized. Our claim is illustrated by means of a well-known economic sequence, the Keynes-Effect (KE).

2. Uncertainty

Under radical *un*certainty the forthcoming results of agents' current decisions will be determined by the values that some economic variables will adopt in the future. In an uncertain scenario these future values are unknown because they do not yet exist (actually in the present they are *in principle unknowable*).

Traditional methodology has agreed that our knowledge is uncertain, in the sense (somewhat different from the one just mentioned) that we can never be sure of the truth-value of statements that say something about the world. It is interesting to note that this limitation (our inability to recognize the truth of an empirical or factual statement, even if it is in fact true) is present even in the weakest scenario (complexity) and even for those factors about which we do have information. Radical uncertainty is much more intractable than its methodological counterpart and is ultimately ontological in nature. How could agents know for certain events that do not exist yet? If the kind of uncertainty related to traditional methodology is unavoidable, it is more so in the case of *radical uncertainty*, which comes from the ontological nature of the economic world.

3. Keynes Effect (KE)[1]

To illustrate our claim we examine the main features of a particularly relevant case of economic process: the so-called *Keynes Effect* (in short KE). Some observations about the role this illustration plays in the argument is in order. First, no attempt to determine which of the many available (and competing) economic theories is the 'correct' one is made here. Fortunately, I do not need to make up my mind about this issue. If any contribution is contained in this book, it is a philosophical reflection concerning what else besides theoretical economic knowledge is needed for regular economic patterns to obtain. I choose KE because the role of both agents' expectations and external interventions are clearly visible in it, but any other economic "regularity" could have been chosen for the present purpose as well. Further, it should be pointed out that I am not claiming to offer a *general* characterization of what an economic process is or is made of. However I believe that the present account could also be relevant for illuminating many other economic processes and the sort of practice that helps to generate economic regularities. To show its main stages let's suppose a market in which both unemployment and flexible wages exist. With unemployment, wages are bid down, marginal costs drop and output expands. However, the extra output cannot be all sold because the marginal propensity to consume is less than 1. Thus, there will be accumulation of inventories and this will lead to price reductions. The change in the price

---

[1] This section largely follows the arguments developed in a co-authored paper (see Ivarola et al., *Economic Thought*, Vol. 2, N° 2, October 2013.

level will lower the demand for active balances, causing the demand for money function to shift and creating an excess supply of money at the prevailing rate of interest. This results in a corresponding excess demand for bonds, with the result that bond prices will increase causing the interest rate to fall (at least until the excess supply of money is channeled into speculative or idle balances). Because the interest rate is a key variable determining investment, the lower rate of interest will encourage higher levels of investment (and of aggregate demand). This leads to higher levels of output and to the elimination of involuntary unemployment.

The idea involved in the notion of mechanism is that it is a sequence of stages that once triggered (i.e. the initial stage is activated), and assuming no interferences in its development, the process continues in a firm and stable way. Thus, in order to reach the *final stage* it is only required that the triggering factor be activated. Apparently, the KE satisfies this condition. In order to show its most crucial steps, the complex process referred to above is often represented in the simplified way depicted below:

$$+\Delta M \longrightarrow -\Delta i \longrightarrow +\Delta I \longrightarrow +\Delta N \longrightarrow +\Delta Y \text{ (KE)}$$

where the expressions $+\Delta X$ and $(-\Delta X)$ mean, respectively, a positive (negative) change in a variable X. KE asserts that when the money supply (M) increases, a decrease in the interest rate (i) will take place (stage I). This change will stimulate investment (I) (stage II) and consequently employment (N) and production (Y) (stage III). KE describes what may be called the 'typical road', because it is the succession of steps that normally prevails. It will be shown however that in practice the situation can be very different, given that the causal connections between economic variables are made possible through human participation at two different levels.

4. Deviations from the typical road

The KE process described above is not isolated, but is part of a broader picture provided by the General Theory, which consists of a set of interrelated sub-processes. Therefore, KE prevails as long as a *ceteris paribus* clause – including all the remaining relevant factors – is met. Hence, the normal prevalence of KE means that changes in those factors are not significant enough to prevent its accomplishment. However, these changes may sometimes be significant. As a consequence, agents modify their course of action, which alters the normal behaviour of KE. In Keynes' words:

> "We have now introduced money into our causal nexus for the first time, and we are able to catch a first glimpse of the way in which changes in the quantity of money work their way into the economic system. If, however, we are tempted to assert that money is the drink which stimulates the system to activity, we must remind ourselves that there may be several slips between the cup and the lip. For whilst an increase in the quantity of money may be expected, cet. par., to reduce the rate of interest, this will not happen if the liquidity-preferences of the public are increasing more than the quantity of money; and whilst a decline in the rate of interest may be expected, cet. par., to increase the volume of investment, this will not happen if the schedule of the marginal efficiency of capital is falling more rapidly than the rate of interest; and whilst an increase in the volume of investment may be expected, cet. par., to increase employment, this may not happen if the propensity to consume is falling off. Finally, if employment increases, prices will rise in a degree partly governed by the shapes of the physical supply functions, and partly by the liability of the wage-unit to rise in terms of money. And when output has increased and prices have risen, the effect of this on liquidity- preference will be to increase the quantity of money necessary to maintain a given rate of interest (Keynes, 1936, p. 155)'.

This situation may be represented through the following schema.

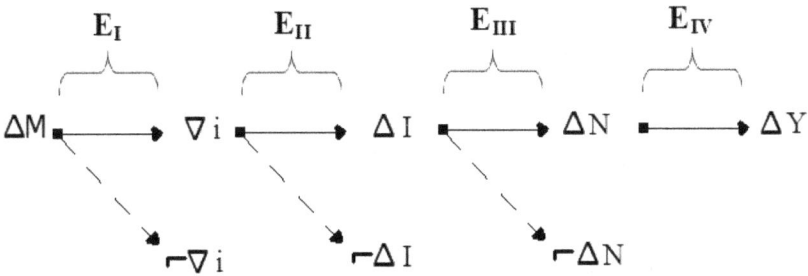

The horizontal arrows denote the KE process, and the diagonal arrows (dotted lines) denote possible exceptions which impede KE to continue its process until the final state. The symbol '¬' means the negation of change in the economic variable. In what follows, we explain the deviations of the KE-process through its respective stages, specifying the conditions in which it is possible to take alternative sides from the standard process. It is argued that these deviations have their origin in the information obtained from the context, which significantly influences the agents' expectations.

First Deviation: no change in the interest rate

According to Keynes' statement, let us suppose that despite the application of an expansionary political economy, the liquidity-preference of the public grows more than the quantity of money. If so, then the monetary policy will have no impact on the interest rate, as people are not going to use that surplus of money to buy goods or bonds. An interesting example of this is the 'liquidity trap'; let us assume that the interest rate is quite low. In this case, agents are waiting for an increase in the interest rate. This is equivalent to saying that they are expecting a decrease in the price of bonds. Therefore, they will not end up buying bonds. Instead, they will prefer to keep their surplus of money (precautionary motive). Hence, an increase in money supply will not bring about significant consequences in the interest rate. It seems that people's reactions are sensitive to two relevant kinds of signals: those coming from an increase in money supply and those coming from the context (different values of interest rates bring about different people's reactions).

Second Deviation: no change in investment

At this stage we must assume that the increase in money supply has successfully reduced the level of interest. Nevertheless, let us suppose that the marginal efficiency of capital is falling more rapidly than the rate of interest (Keynes, 1936). If so, firms will be reluctant to invest. We analyze this case through two examples. In the first one, let us suppose that there are no good expectations about future sales. *Ceteris paribus*, there is a decrease in the marginal efficiency of capital. If this decrease is greater than the decrease in *i*, then though credits may be cheaper, this signal will not impact on the amount of investment. This is due to low expectations in future sales, which has an important effect on the expected profitability of projects. In the second example, let us suppose that agents disagree about the future behaviour of the interest rate. If most of them think that it will go down for a while, then they will not invest, because new entrepreneurs will be able to benefit from even lower interest rates, increasing their profitability.

Third Deviation: no change in total employment

In order to understand this stage, it is necessary to introduce Keynes' distinction between primary employment in the investment industries (N2) and total employment (N). Let's suppose that there is an increase in investment that brings about an increase in employment in the investment industries (N2). Through the Kahn' multiplier, the increase in N2 will mean a higher increase in N.

Nevertheless, the expectations formed in this step not only depend on the information that N2 has increased but also on the estimation that the consumer sector has about the marginal propensity to consume. Specifically, total employment will increase as long as this sector does not expect a drop in the marginal propensity to consume. In this sense, let us assume that the marginal propensity to consume decreases – for instance, as a result of propaganda in time of war in favor of restricting individual consumption. In such a case, firms producing consumer goods will receive, on one hand, a signal of higher employment in the investment industries (an increase in N2), but on the other, an imminent reduction in consumption which could negatively affect their expectation of future sales. Consequently, they could find no incentive to hire additional workers.

5. The underlying structure of Keynes Effect

Social processes involve two kinds of *elements*: those which transmits information (for instance, the actual state of economic variables or the changes they show), and the *human* entity (economic agents), who receives and interprets the information sent by the transmitter entity, and reacts to the information they receive. Such reactions usually bring about changes in other economic variables. The process that links together all these pieces is outlined in the following chart.

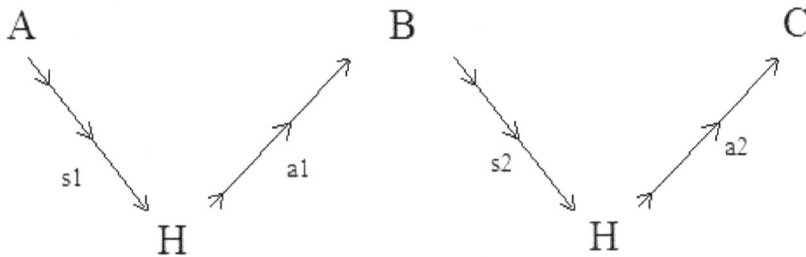

This means that the actual state (or a change in state) of an entity A – conceived as a starting condition – provides information (s1) for agents (H), who receive it, interpret it, and consequently react in a certain way (a1), which generates a change in the state of another entity, B. This result functions as new information (s2) for agents (not necessarily the same agents who generate the latter response), who receive it, interpret it and consequently react, developing a new response (a2), which modifies the state of the entity C. This change in C would represent the final stage of the process.

The KE process fits fairly well into this schema. A simplified representation of the underlying structure of the first stage of KE is this:

$+\Delta M \rightarrow\rightarrow H \rightarrow\rightarrow -\Delta i$

Here, we identify three main components of the process: (1) *changes in economic variables* (in this case an increase in money supply), (2) *agents* (who receive this information), and (3) the *responses* they enact (which contribute by generating a change in another economic variable: the interest rate). Agents are *active* in two different senses: first, they receive signals from changes in variables and interpret them; second, based on the information received, they react, adopting some decisions of economic relevance. The arrows drawn at both sides of H represent this complex nature of human action in a social process. However, the situation is a little bit more complex. The significance or meaning that individuals attach to changes in economic variables depends on the specific *contexts* in which they take place. The information that carries with it an increase in money supply is different under full employment than in conditions in which unemployment is high. The same change in a variable (say a reduction of 1% in the interest rate) sends a different message to individuals in different contexts. This is why fiscal policies are ineffective under full employment but successful when unemployment goes up. It is important to be aware that the relevant context that agents take into account to make decisions is not only made of strictly economic variables. Institutions, rules, and political considerations are also important when adopting economic decisions.

Other crucial components of economic processes are the *expectations* that individuals form about future changes in some relevant economic variables. They are formed under the guide of the information received. Expectations and responses are strongly related to each other: once individuals form their expectations they make decisions on this basis. Thus, we can say that *responses* developed by economic agents are triggered by expectations. The role that expectations play makes them susceptible of *interventions* by several economic actors (corporations, political parties, Media) all along the process. They can do it directly (making public declarations in order to form agents' opinions) or indirectly (operating on the relevant context in order to influence agent´s expectations according to their particular interests). Taking all this into account, we express the causal structure of the processes in the following picture:

Economic processes

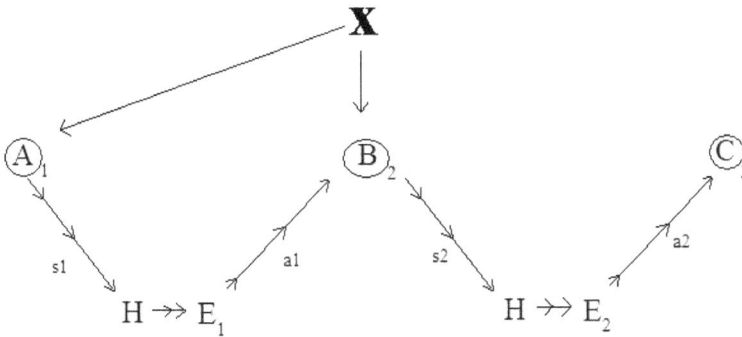

Here A, B, and C represent a constellation of institutional, political and economic variables (which may be designed as a socio-economic environment), and X represent the actors' interventions intended to shape the relevant context. A certain change in A sends a signal (s1) to the individual (H). Using this information he forms expectations (E1) which play a crucial role in determining the response (a1), which, in turn, in combination with a second round of economic actors' interventions, contributes to an alteration of B, and so on. Within a socio-economic environment these are the strictly economic variables that agents ultimately want to affect. This shows the interplay of agents' decisions and actors' interventions in the conformation of economic processes.

Given the discomfort that the academic audience feels regarding laws, the processual approach advanced in this paper seems to be an appealing notion that promises to be useful to understand social and economic contexts.

Agents' expectations have a decisive role in economic processes. On one hand, expectations are a key target that should be intervened on so as to insure the direction of the process. To the extent that some specific arrangement of expectations leading from a change in an economic variable to a change in another variable is known, the pertinent interventions will be addressed to guarantee a background of information that promotes the shaping of those expectations. The other key target to be intervened is the environment (i.e., institutions, regulations, political climate, etc.). Even if economics have focused on Government's interventions many other agents constantly interfere trying to influence the economic process. And they do so both on agents' expectations and on the socio-economic environment.

Two different kinds of knowledge sustain this sort of intervention. Firstly, *theoretical* knowledge is needed in order to know which economic variables have to be manipulated. Nonetheless, *practical* knowledge is also needed in order to operate on expectations, so that agents' responses are performed in the desired and expected way. Let us take the example of KE: nobody expects that the final goal (an increase in employment) will be achieved spontaneously. Instead, such a goal is perceived as the result of a set of interventions at each stage of the mechanism. In this juncture, we should recall the difference between knowing 'what' and knowing 'how'. In politics, not only do you need to know *what* to do, but also *how* to do it. The necessary skills for an adequate intervention combine both types of knowledge. For instance, focusing on State's intervention it is often recognized that in order to increase investment both the interest rate has to be lowered and entrepreneurs' uncertainty about the future ought to be dissipated. Reducing the interest rate is a step that can be taken in a rather direct way. However, dissipating uncertainty is somehow more difficult to achieve because it depends on a complex set of expectations. In particular, it presupposes a kind of knowledge that, properly speaking, is not scientific knowledge. On the contrary, it requires knowing *how to* manage peoples' expectations.

6. Processes vs mechanisms. How to distinguish them?

As we saw in the preceding chapter the concept of "mechanism" is usually evoked by theoretical economists. But the sequences of events in which uncertainty and conflict of interests prevail, as in the case of KE, are not mechanisms! We are going to offer now additional arguments against the idea that the concept of mechanism is significant within the scope of economics. Our notion of "intervenible and open ended economic processes" must be distinguished from the usual notions of "mechanism" (Woodward, Glenann) and "nomological machine" (Cartwright). We will designate both approaches as "processual" and "mechanistic", respectively, and will defend the first of them. A problem that we face is how to differentiate both concepts (processes and mechanisms) in a conceptually adequate way, and to argue why the first is preferable.

Both approaches differ in the way in which they conceive the function of the interventions. The mechanistic view assigns them two different fundamental roles: a) to activate mechanisms' triggering conditions; b) to avoid the interference of external factors that could prevent their normal operation. The first intervention is internal to the mechanism and the second one is external to it. In order to illustrate this difference we consider the following sequence S:

$$a \rightarrow b \rightarrow c \rightarrow d \qquad\qquad (S)$$

That S is a mechanism means that its "parts" - a, b, etc. - and the relations between them are stable. Only the intervention I on the mechanism is made at the beginning (over state a). I is said to provide the "triggering conditions". Once started the regular conduct of the sequence is guaranteed by means of a particular type of external intervention in order to "shield" the sequence from disturbing influences coming from outside.

The mechanistic approach reasons as if, once shot, the sequence of steps had its own dynamics, provided it is not disturbed. This means two things. First, if an intervention is made in order to obtain a, it also obtains b, c and d (provided that S is isolated). The intervention is limited to the initial step (triggering condition) and no further interventions are needed to obtain the remaining steps of the sequence.

Processes do not fit such description. Agents' expectations are part of the sequences of economic phenomena. But expectations do not have a given content (there are no "natural" or "pure" expectations). A change in an economic factor does not generate in agent S a defined expectation, discernible beforehand (perhaps by means of empirical and theoretical resources), which leads that agent to act in a certain well defined way, so that phenomenon b is generated. There is no such inevitability. This is the kernel of the phenomenon called *subjectivism*: there is no causal connection between a certain set of information that the individual receives and the expectations he forms on that basis. This gap happens because nobody knows how is the agent going to process the information he receives (what meaning is he going to assign to it). Nevertheless, although the received information does not strictly determine the agents' expectations it certainly contributes to their formation. More particularly, any kind of intervention on agents' expectations helps to their formation. Expectations are not given, nor do they have a "natural" content. They are something to be partly constructed by interventions. These interventions are also an integral part of the sequences of social events (processes).

The mechanistic approach is "essentialist", in the sense that it assumes that social processes typically follow a "natural" course. It is clear that this is not the case, since the expectations that contribute to generate those processes are not those that an agent "naturally" would form, but those that were product of the subjective interpretation that agents make of the general situation in which they are, and of the concurrent efforts of many different kinds of lobbyists to influence and control the process in order to fulfill their interests.

The discourse in terms of laws or mechanisms neglects the fact that social sequences are internally constituted (constructed) by deliberate action of many lobbyists. This way of talking also neglects that processes' internal dynamics are constantly influenced from outside (any sort of external interference is discarded by incorporating the shielding condition). These convenient assumptions allow the reduction of social processes to mechanisms, which are conceived as natural regularities that operate behind (on the back of) agents' consciousness. Those who believe that such a reduction is legitimate also believe that economic science would be needed to discover the main steps of the sequence and their remote effects once it is shot. Let us consider this thesis now.

7. Unexpected and inevitable consequences

An idea compatible with the mechanistic approach in economics is that unexpected consequences of our present actions exist (consequences that can be discovered beforehand by means of appropriate knowledge).

Economic processes

> "No very deep knowledge of economics is usually needed for grasping the immediate effects of a measure; but the task of economics is to foretell the remoter effects, and so to allow us to avoid such acts as attempts to remedy a present ill by sowing the seeds of a much greater ill for the future".
> (Ludwig von Mises, *The Theory of Money and Credit*)

The idea is that when doing A in t0, an interventionist hopes to obtain B in a later time t1, but the scientific theory (some type of knowledge superior to the one of the practical man) reveals that after a long chain of consequences the result will be different (or even opposed) from the one aimed in t0. It is interesting that Mises emphasizes the case in which the chain of consequences is long. It is respect to the long run that, presumably, economic science acquires advantage over common sense or practical knowledge, since the immediate consequences are obvious, according to him. Hayek and Popper have also claimed that the task (or at least one of the main tasks) of social sciences is to find out these consequences.

Note first that "consequence" is a term taken from the context of logic. In an argument given the premises certain consequences (inexorably) follow. Given the premises, their consequences could have been unnoticed in advance but they cannot be avoided. Outside the domain of logical reasoning, however, it is more appropriate to use the notions of "causes" and "effects". But now the situation changes. It is true that given the cause, its effects would have to "inexorably" follow if the referred notion of cause were of the "simpliciter" type. But usually what we denominate "cause" is only one of the many influencing factors that for some reason we selected from a set of concurrent circumstances. In these cases it is more reasonable to adopt the notion of "relative" cause, that according to Cartwright can be represented thus:

$$(C . N) \; c \rightarrow E$$

Here C is the selected cause in which the analysis focuses, N is the remaining relevant environment, E is the effect and "$c \rightarrow$" is a symbol for causal relation. Now the occurrence of a causal factor C does not guarantee the occurrence of effect E. C causes E if conditions N are fulfilled. If *a posteriori* of C some lobbyists intervene adopting diverse measures in order to transform context N (which includes expectations) into a different context N', E may not happen after all. The moral of this analysis is that the (logical) consequences are inevitable, but the predicted effects can be avoided (if some agent judges them undesirable and acts appropriately). In the domain of deductive relations, if a set of premises P implies a consequence Q, any "intervention" like the addition of new premises is totally ineffective to avoid Q. But material interventions can contribute to transform the resulting effects in the case of causal relations.

The notion of open processes illustrated in this chapter rejects the idea of fatalism, which is presupposed in the search of mechanisms that reveal ex–ante the course of future events (the idea that if an intervention makes X in t0, inevitably Y will happen in t1, although Y has not been wished nor imagined by anybody at t0). Maybe such mechanisms exist, but if this were the case examples should be provided, and those who defend their existence would contribute to a better understanding of them if they explained the conditions of their exceptional occurrence.

The anti-fatalist approach that we propose for social processes rescues two basic ideas: a) The future is not predetermined in the present (strictly speaking, it does not exist yet); b) The future course of social events is largely in our hands (it will be fruit of the successive decisions of agents, which partly depend on the conflicting influences of different economic actors who behave like lobbyists).

As we maintain in the last chapters of this book, theoretical practice makes a vital contribution to the construction of that future, identifying sequences of feasible events. But it is important to notice that the wished result still must be constructed (it will not come on its own, in an spontaneous and inexorable way).

8. Thinking processes with an eye on Lego

A concept similar to that of "mechanism" is the concept of "nomological machine" (NM; Cartwright):

Economic processes

> "It is a fixed (enough) arrangement of components, or
> factors, with stable (enough) capacities that in the right sort
> of stable (enough) environment will, with repeated operation,
> give rise to the kind of regular behavior that we represent in
> our scientific laws". (Cartwright 1999b: 50)

The active presence of a NM is what ensures the occurrence of stable empirical regularities. Certain types of inputs enter the machine and a well-defined output ensues. A paradigmatic example of nomological machine is that which automatically expends beverages and cookies (let´s call it expending machine). The user activates the machine (inserts a suitable form of currency and presses the corresponding button) and after a repetitive series of internal processes within the machine he receives the awaited product. The NM has three characteristics: (a) stable parts, (b) stable relations between its parts and (c) isolation from potentially disturbing factors.

A central problem for conceiving social processes like "mechanisms" and "nomological machines" is that in social processes the aspects (b) and (c) usually are not fulfilled. In order to analyze these failures we shall consider first a rather fantastic variation of the old and dear expending machine. We will call it homuncular machine (HM).

A HM contains physical parts (material objects), intelligent or independent parts (the homunculi) and relations between the parts. An expending machine that contains amusing little men in its interior would be a machine of this type. Without the little men the machine behaves normally (this happens for instance when they are sleeping): a client introduces a token, pushes the corresponding button, the mechanism activates and after a certain number of steps serves the chosen product. But such a HM can disappoint the client, since the little men can cause the awaited sequence not to happen. They could stop it completely or interfere so that the process results in something the client did not wish. Unlike the usual mechanisms in the New Mechanistic Literature, this HM does not work in a foreseeable way once activated (even being isolated). It contains, so to speak, an innovating principle in its interior (inside). How would any sorts of stable regularities arise in such system?

If this illustration sounds too fantastic, think of a boy playing with Lego. The game has a fixed number n of pieces. But the relations between the pieces are variable, in the sense that piece 4 can be connected with piece 3 or with many others, and they in turn can be connected in many diverse ways. It is the boy who decides how to assemble the pieces as he plays. Suppose the game allows constructing k results (tables, cars, boats, etc.). Can it be said beforehand which of them the boy will construct at the end of the game? Surely not, unless he shows a sort of repetitious behavior doing the same over and over again.

The HM (expending machine or a boy playing Lego) can be externally influenced (intervened) in a more active way than simply "shooting it". The intervention now attempts to influence the decisions of the "homunculi". Let us return to the example of the boy playing with his Lego set. Let us suppose that his father is present. Can he influence the way in which the boy assembles the pieces? Surely he can, but he could well fail. The boy must be persuaded by his father if he wishes the pieces to be assembled in a certain (well determined) way. The trio father-boy-Lego conforms a very simple system, in which there is just one active principle (the boy) dedicated to assemble Lego parts and only one "interventionist" (the father), who strives to influence the preferences and decisions of the boy.

Other systems can be much more complex: one of them can have many children sharing the pieces of a Lego set and assembling "something" in a concurrent way. The activity can also have more than one observer, each striving to induce the children to make different decisions. As long as there are more children operating and more fathers lobbying for different assemblages (i.e., competing with each other to exert influence on the children), the final result of the process is more uncertain than it was before. The "intelligent parts" of the system (the children) do not respond in an invariable way to the stimuli they receive. They interpret them. And they can do it in many different ways. Their interpretations are intervenible, but the success of the interventions is not ensured. How could stable patterns arise in such a scenario?

There is one important difference between observers and players: the fathers can influence the behavior of the children (but the inverse is not the case). There exists then an asymmetry of power between both groups. But no asymmetry of knowledge occurs, because nobody can know beforehand what the final result will be. In the most interesting case the observers can have different goals (aiming at different results). This means that they compete with each other to influence the decisions of the children (and the configuration of the final result). They could have diverse skills in persuasion. But none of them can be sure what the result will be (all are uncertain about this point). More precisely, they are uncertain about two things: a) what attitude will the children adopt in face of the pressures; b) which of the diverse influences (or which particular composition of them) will prevail. Evidently we are very far from the case of the expending machine.

Although it is not possible to be known what "apparatus" will result once the children have connected all the set, the many possible combinations from the available pieces can be anticipated. The number of possible resulting apparatuses, as well as the ways that lead to them, can be huge, but in principle they can be known. The situation could be depicted as a set of sequences that adopts the format of a tree of possibilities. Although at each step the tree is open-ended, the construction undergoes restrictions that neither the inventiveness of the children nor the intervention of their parents can avoid. The number of pieces is given and also their format, something that prevents that a given piece may be assembled with any other.

Although there is uncertainty under two forms (what decisions the children will make and what influence the parents will have), in this scenario a significant amount of knowledge is available from the beginning: we know the pieces that will be assembled and the restrictions that govern the said assembly. For that reason, in principle each of the multiple complete sequences can be anticipated (as well as their corresponding resulting apparatuses). In a more creative scenario, it could be allowed that at each step of their play children construct their own pieces (or they add external pieces to the given Lego set), and add them to the ones already available. It could also allow changes in the composition of the sets of children and parents (the entrance of new participants and the exit of others previously present). This would eliminate the two previous restrictions and would cause the sequences of assembly and the final results to become completely unpredictable.

The designed mechanisms that were examined in the previous chapter differ substantially from the systems composed by many children and many parents, coming together in a joint construction effort using a Lego set. In the three cases (PL, MD and RAS) one verifies asymmetry of knowledge in favor of the interventionists, and a substantial homogeneity in their interests. In all these cases there is a group of designers who has generated the conditions to orient the choices of the decision makers. The revolt of the "homunculi" is deactivated and their creativity is circumscribed and controlled.

In this sense, such mechanisms look much more like the selling machine than the game of Lego, where the lobbyists are not necessarily a homogenous group, but can have different and even opposing interests. On the other hand, they exert their influence continuously throughout the process. The capacity of each sub-group to influence the players' decisions is not uniformly distributed and can vary along the time, and new actors can join in whereas others leave the game. All the time the preeminence is in dispute and the result is uncertain. The moral I would like to convey is that economic processes are much more like (the complex version of) Lego than mechanisms and machines.

Part III

How to conceive rationality, testing, learning and theoretical practice given uncertainty

Introduction

A central tenet of this book is that the "real" nature of the world imposes restrictions to individuals' knowledge. The (objective) features of the intended target are central to deciding whether it is possible to use theories and models to obtain scientific (that is to say, relevant and reliable) knowledge of it and what type of technologies can be successfully implemented on these grounds. In particular, this book is interested in clarifying the conditions to achieve this goal. Some considerations about these issues were advanced in Chapter Four, but the principle that asserts the priority of ontological considerations also applies when approaching epistemic issues. Particularly, the possibility of deciding rationally, when open ended processes subject to interventions and pervaded by radical uncertainty are being considered.

The main claims of the following chapters are: (a) given some key *ontological features* of economic processes (described in Chapter Five) agents cannot behave according to well grounded ex-ante rationality, unless rationality is understood in a *subjectivist and coherentist* sense; (b) furthermore, if some reasonable ontological and epistemic *beliefs* are attributed to economic agents, they also *cannot* behave rationally in a subjectivist and coherentist sense; (c) and, if uncertainty reigns, the use of other essential concepts in economics, like *testing* and *learning*, that are not conceptually problematic in conditions in which certainty or risk is assumed, also require analysis and justification. The whole concept of *theoretical practice* should also be rethought if economic processes are the target.

Rethinking theoretical economics and philosophy of economics

Chapter 6
Rationality

Although assuming radical uncertainty is not applicable to all economic scenarios, we suppose that it is valid in a great variety of cases (whose scope deserves to be investigated). There are two basic notions of individual rationality. First, there is a subjectivist and coherentist notion of rational behavior which conceives "rationality" as consistency among agents' beliefs, preferences and actions. This is the one involved in Expected Utility Theory. Second, rationality is seen as a sort of calculation driving decisions that precedes the realization of their future consequences. I call it *well-grounded ex-ante rationality*. "Well grounded" because it is supposed to be founded on a calculation that takes into account the best available evidence. "Ex-ante" because its results will be available *after* the decision is made. Thus understood, the rationality of a decision can be recognized *before* its results are manifest.[1] This is the kind of rationality that Keynes had in mind.

In this chapter I claim that assuming that rationality is of the well-grounded ex-ante type, agents cannot behave rationally under uncertainty. However, scholars disagree and following Keynes' remarks maintain that even in those circumstances there is room for rational action. They offer three different arguments in support of this claim: (a) agents can employ induction in order to form "rational beliefs" about future events; (b) agents can perform some kind of rational economic calculation; (c) agents are able to decide rationally

---

[1] Rationality, understood as well grounded and ex-ante, cannot be identified with efficiency. In a game of chance a lucky guy can win frequently, but this fact does not turn his choices into rational decisions. If rationality is conceived in this way those decisions that an individual takes in time t0 cannot be judged by their consequences at a later time tj. What really matters is their relation with the antecedent evidence available in t0.

following a number of "techniques" or conventions.[2] I will contest the validity of these arguments.

As a reference, we examine first Expected Utility Theory (EUT), which has been developed for risky conditions, and allows the allocation of subjective probabilities to the occurrence of unknown states of the world, and identifies rationality with having a consistent *system* of beliefs and preferences.

1. Expected Utility Theory *(EUT)*

An agent confronts a decision problem when he must choose between alternative actions that will have different consequences. In some cases, the decision is simple, because the agent can judge beforehand and in an objective way which is the best option. Usually in these cases the subject makes (carries out) some type of calculation that allows him to recognize the best alternative among the available ones. This is the typical situation in conditions of certainty or risk. Under risky conditions the result cannot be anticipated for sure but only with a certain objectively determinable probability.

For instance, consider two urns, A and B, each of them containing ten balls. In the first nine are white and one black, and there are five white and five black in the second. Suppose a person is asked to pick up a ball from one of the urns. He will receive $1 if the ball is white and $2 if it is black. Which urn will the rational agent choose? In this case *objective* probabilities about the payoffs he will receive in any case may be attached to both alternatives. The action that is rational/irrational may be perfectly identified beforehand in these circumstances and one can demonstrate to a decision maker that his choice is optimal/not optimal.

---

[2] These three strategies find some support in Keynes' work. The first is developed in his Theory of probability, the second is described in Chapter 11 of his General Theory, and the latest is also suggested in GT but it is made fully explicit in his article "The general theory of employment" published in 1937.

Rationality

EUT extends the above approach and posits that agents may also choose in a rational way between alternatives of a very different kind. Let us suppose that an entrepreneur S, who has a certain sum of money, say U.S. dollars (USD) 2, faces the two following options. Course of action A: If he invests in a zone of conflict, he can obtain a profit of USD 10 with probability p1; otherwise he loses his investment completely. Course of action B: If he invests in a politically stable zone he can earn USD 5, with probability p2, and USD 2 in the worst case. The rational decision for S is to choose that lottery that has greater expected utility for him. If the monetary remunerations of the options are given, as in this case (but remember that they are mere subjective estimations: other entrepreneurs could well consider completely different values), the decision is going to depend on the values that S assigns to p1 and p2. In particular, S must choose between the two following lotteries:

A: (10, -2, p1) or B: (5, 2, p2)

Which means that if he picks A he will obtain USD 10 with probability p1 or he will lose USD 2 with probability 1-p1. The expected utilities of each lottery are these:

EU (A) = p1 (10) + (1-p1) (-2)
EU (B) = p2 (5) + (1-p2) (2)

The only restriction that S faces in assigning probabilities to the prizes of each lottery is that their sum must be exactly equal to 1. But as much as he complies with this restriction, he has freedom to assign to each probability the value he wishes. This means that if he thinks that p1 = 0,5 and p2 = 0,2, EU (A) will be 4 and EU (B) will be 2,6, and S will choose alternative A because it is better ranked than B. But if he assigns other values to p1 or p2 he could select the alternative B.

The procedure does not contain any criterion to decide when S is guessing right in his attribution of probabilities and when he is mistaken (except in the case in which the requirement of consistency is violated). This vision of rationality is coherentist and subjectivist. It is *coherentist* because it imposes formal restrictions to the *sets* of preferences and beliefs that an agent can have, not to the elements of these sets. And it is *subjectivist* because the assigned probabilities as well as the ranking of the prizes and lotteries can be anything: as long as the agent is coherent he can choose any alternative without acting irrationally.

2. Keynes' criticism

For mainstream economics agents' decisions are taken in conditions of certainty or risk, which involves strong commitments about the knowledge and logic capacities of individuals, who might be able to form a complete order of preferences and maximize. In his *Treatise on Probability* (TP) Keynes explicitly presents this view and explores, contradicting Hume, the admissibility of non-demonstrative inferences. This fact, in conjunction with other expressions of his *General Theory* (GT) has led some people to think that in Keynes' view economic agents could act rationally under uncertainty, although in a weaker and different sense of rationality than that assumed in mainstream economics. Taking Keynes's words at face value, many post-Keynesians are ready to sustain this view along three different lines of argument.

The first one is based on TP, where Keynes looked for logical rules of partial implication between sentences which could be used in the formation of what he called *rational* beliefs. Nothing is said there about economics or economic thinking. Keynes' analysis was carried out in a very *general* level and aimed at constructing what we may call now an inductive logic.

The second line of argument starts from GT and his article "The General Theory of employment" (1937), where Keynes expanded his earlier views on induction to economics. He said, indeed, that economic theory should abandon the usual epistemological assumptions involved in classical theory and picture agents in a realist manner, facing genuine uncertainty and reasoning from (usually very limited) partial knowledge.

There is some continuity between TP and GT: in both books, the Humean idea which identifies knowledge, or rational knowledge, with deductive reasoning is rejected. If there is a difference between them in this respect it should be looked for at the level of analysis. In TP Keynes sustained a general thesis about the possibility of rational individual behavior in conditions in which the bases for reasoning (the premises) are insufficient to reach a conclusion; in GT, it seems, he claimed the applicability of this thesis to the particular case of an expert investor operating in the stock market, who in some way could compare rationally the costs and prospective yields of his actual decisions.[3] Although this second thesis is considerably weaker than the first one, it depends on the possibility of performing the probability calculation explored in TP.

Some post-Keynesians have supported the rationality of economic agents under uncertainty advancing an argument that does not rest on the possibility of an inductive logic or the possibility of the economic calculation. These authors recognize that no valid calculation is possible at all under uncertainty. But they believe that even under these circumstances agents are able to behave rationally following certain rules or conventions.

Summing up. Based on Keynes' explicit thinking there are then three avenues to defend agents' rationality under uncertainty. The first attempt expands the notion of rationality letting induction be included in it; the second tries to show that investors can behave in a rational manner performing some kind of calculation; and the third supposes that it may be rational to follow some practical rules or conventions. In the following sections I shall revise critically each one of these assertions.

3. Inductive logic

Although Keynes appreciates Hume's work very much, his understanding of the Humean position regarding induction was mistaken. To Keynes "Hume showed ... not that inductive methods ... were false, but that their validity had

---

[3] This is the view of those post-keynesians (Carabelli, 1988) who think that in his *General Theory* Keynes simply applied his earlier views on probability to economics. The "continuity" thesis is problematic and has recently been criticized (Davis, 1994; Cottrell, 1993). It will not be examined here. In an original version of this chapter, I attributed the continuity thesis to Rod O'Donnell (1989), but recently he makes clear to me that this is not his position.

never been established".[4] I think he is mistaken. In Keynes's view Hume had merely identified a *de facto* limitation in inductive reasoning, when the truth is that Hume sustained a much stronger thesis, which points at the existence of an insurmountable difficulty in induction. Elaborating on this faulty interpretation Keynes worried all through TP, trying to find a solution to – what he thought – was Hume's problem.[5]

In so doing Keynes distinguished between belief, *rational* belief and certain knowledge. Let *h* be a hypothesis. Mere believing in *h* does not need any foundation whatsoever (in this sense it is analogous to "prophecy" for standard methodology). The belief in *h* is *rational* if it is supported by an available evidence *e*. Finally, one has certain knowledge of *h* when one of the two following circumstances is fulfilled: a) *h* is known directly (it is self-evident) or b) *h* is known indirectly (*e* is known directly and *h* is logically entailed from *e*). Rational belief involves some probability relation (*partial entailment*) between *e* and *h*. To Keynes this probability is objective and is "knowable" by intuition. In TP Keynes shows, indeed, that under exceptional circumstances it is possible to objectively form probability judgments like *h1/e* > *h2/e* (which means that given *e*, *h1* is at least as probable as *h2*).

Suppose Keynes is right and there really exists an objective world of partial logical relations between sentences (this is the platonic ontology that Keynes takes from Moore).[6] Suppose also that these probabilities can be known by

---

[4] In Keynes's view, Hume merely showed that "while it is true that past experience gives rise to a psychological anticipation of some events rather than others, no ground has been given for the validity of this superior anticipation" (quoted in Meeks, 2003, p. 27).

[5] Curiously enough, Keynes's interpretation of Hume's argument is quite similar to Mill's. "To the modern reader, the phrase 'the justification of induction' brings to mind Hume's famous attack on the soundness of inductive reasoning. The importance of his treatment of induction is scarcely disputed even by those who are loath to believe his startling skeptical conclusion that there can be no such thing as a sound inductive argument; for it is normally accepted that that claim must be refuted and not merely ignored. Yet the refutation of Hume was not an objective of Mill, though he did regard himself in Book III as justifying inductive inference. Indeed, Mill seems not to have grasped what Hume's problem was, and his chief concern was to explain how inference from particulars to particulars – the standard pattern of valid reasoning-despite its appearance of slightness was really the only form of inference which science either needed to, or could, admit" (Scarre, 1998, p. 116).

[6] Keynes pushed Moore's argument much further, because the latter did not think probabilities were unique objective entities.

intuition. The problem is that Keynes also asserted the radical subjectivity of knowledge, according to which every individual has his own appreciation of the assumed objective relations. This means that even if Keynes was right and the probability relations exist and were objective in an ontological way, the probability judgments formed by individuals would be entirely subjective.[7] Even if it were true that $h1/e$ > $h2/e$, some individuals could nevertheless intuit the opposite.

This combination of objective and subjective views, led to Keynes' idea that even if the agents cannot calculate in the mathematical sense, they can "work out" in a weaker sense: starting from the available evidence they can posit (in an arbitrary way) some probabilities to different hypothesis. In what follows we will distinguish between calculate (in the mathematical sense) and "work out" (in the sense developed on the *Treatise*).

Subjectivity may also be introduced through the notion of "weight" of an argument. Thus, if $e3$ is a piece of relevant information for $h1$, then ($h1/e1, e3$) has more weight than ($h1/e1$). It does not mean, however, that ($h1/e1, e3$) > ($h1/e1$). A stronger partial relation between premises and conclusion allows for a conclusion with lower (not higher) probability. On occasion, it may happen that the weight of the arguments individuals are able to form is so low that they have near zero confidence in the probability assigned to the conclusion, so they are ready to change their judgment in face of minus variations in the available information. This accounts for the extremely fragile nature of probability judgments.

The usual way to escape from the troubles of subjectivism is to posit the existence of a shared human nature, which entails that in spite of individual differences, given certain circumstances people arrive at similar consequences as long as they have "normal" intellectual capacities. This view is espoused in one of Keynes's earlier drafts (Miscellanea Ethica, 1905).

---

[7] "What we know and what probability we can attribute to our rational beliefs is, therefore, subjective in the sense of being relative to the individual" (Keynes, quoted in McCann, 2003, p. 42).

"It is plain that the idea and the emotion appropriate to any given sensation are partly dependent on the nature and the past history of the individual who feels. This is obvious enough; we ought not to all have precisely similar states in similar physical circumstances; common sense and the commandments are agreed on that. But we can in many cases abstract that element which ought to vary from man to man. Assuming the approximate uniformity of human organs, we can often say what, apart from peculiar circumstances, a man ought to think and feel –not indeed what he can think and feel– that will always depend upon his nature and his past" (quoted in Carabelli, 2003, pp. 222-223).

Quoting this passage Carabelli finds it sufficient to avert the threat of subjectivism. As she asserts, "although Keynes allowed a role for both psychological and subjective influences on individual judgment, he also supposed that one could say what an individual should reasonably think and feel on the grounds that there exists an 'approximate uniformity of human organs'. This notion of human mind and thought underlies Keynes's thinking in *A Treatise on Probability*". (Carabelli, 2003, p. 223). This strategy is not new and has been used in economics at least since Mill.[8]

However, it is unlikely that Keynes remained consistent with all his sayings through his life as Carabelli assumes to be the case. Besides, it is one thing to record Keynes' words and another to find them sustainable. The idea of a shared human nature is unclear, and is at best a working hypothesis, which must be elaborated to acquire a clear meaning. What is needed is not just to register Keynes claims but to assess their validity. Even worse, the appeal to a common human nature seems to be inconsistent with his recognition of the

---

[8] See the way in which Mill sustained the idea that we are able to know, in a completely a-priori manner, the decisions taken by a King with absolute power (Mill, 1995, pp. 55-56). More generally, it was asserted that the actions of any human being can be understood "only because the object of our study has a mind of a structure similar to our own" (Hayek, 1979, p. 48). So "to speak of a mind with a structure fundamentally different from our own, or to claim that we can observe changes in the basic structure of the human mind is not only to claim what is impossible: it is a meaningless statement" (Hayek, 1979, p. 135).

unavoidable role of subjectivity. The tension generated can be appreciated in Keynes' following remark:

> "We cannot speak of knowledge absolutely – only of the knowledge of a particular person. Other parts of knowledge – knowledge of the axioms of logic, for example – may seem more objective. But we must admit I think, that this too is relative to the constitution of the human mind, and the constitution of the human mind may vary in some degree from man to man. What is self-evident to me and what I really know, may be only a probable belief to you, or may form no part of your rational beliefs at all. And this may be true not only of such things as my existence, but of some logical axioms also" (quoted in McCann, 2003, p. 41-42).

It will be interesting to establish what individuals who are allowed to differ even about the basic rules of formal logic can have in common! Whatever the solution to this puzzle may be, the fact remains that some post-Keynesians do share vague suspicions about the value of standard logic, which have origins in (and they believe supported by) Keynes' own expressions like the ones just quoted. Nowadays Sheila Dow and Victoria Chick are in the forefront of those who contribute to this attitude. However, their rejection of what they call "classical" logic and their vindication of a different "human" logic is merely rhetoric as long as they are unable to show what this alternative logic is exactly about.

Neither Chick nor Dow seem prepared to defend induction openly, since they reject dualistic thinking and closely follow the precepts of critical realism[9]. Other post-Keynesians who do not have such constraints have taken in their hands Keynes' mandate and looked for some form of justification for inductive reasoning. Meeks, for instance, uses two different arguments in favor of inductive-based behavior. The first one is founded on the coherence between an action and its underlying beliefs. He argues that, "Keynes views actions as rational if they are justified with respect to the beliefs it is reasonable for the agent to form on the available information –

---

[9] The dismissal of both deduction and induction may be found in Lawson's *Economics and Reality*.

recognizing that sometimes this will be subsequently proven to have been misleading" (Meeks, 2003, p. 31).

His description is faulty, because the identification of which belief "is reasonable for the agent to form on the available information" presupposes that the problem of induction has already been solved, which is precisely what is being discussed. Besides, to call "rational" those actions that are "justified" by such beliefs assumes, again, that induction is not problematic. Even if these defects in the formulation of the thesis were fixed, what Meeks describes is quite analogous to situational logic's rationality, which only requires coherence between beliefs, aims and actions, and was appropriated from neoclassical theory. This rationality is weaker (and less significant) than the one Keynes attempted to elaborate in his "Treatise on Probability".

Despite its weakness, this void rationality has some supporters. O´Donnell, for instance, states that uncertainty "does not, of itself, imply irrationality. Rational individuals adapt to their circumstances, and will thus adopt new forms of behavior, forms which I have grouped under the heading of 'weak rationality'. This involves such modes of behavior as the following of social customs, conventions, rules-of-thumb or apparently better-informed opinion, or of allowing more arbitrary procedures such as coin-tossing or pure caprice to decide" (O'Donnell, 1991, p. 81). Later on I make an assessment of the behavior guided by customs and conventions, but it should be clear from now what may be the value of tossing a coin or letting whims command our choices. It is always possible to weaken still further the notion of rationality so that any action may be considered rational. I think this would be a high price to pay for rescuing agents' rationality from the threat of uncertainty.

The second strategy used by Meeks in favor of induction relies in the function attributed to this kind of inference. As he argues, "if taking past experience as our guide is a convention 'none of us could possibly do without', then at least it cannot be unreasonable in the sense that we should *give it up*" (Meeks, 2003, p. 31).[10] It is an odd argument and adds more

---

[10] The expression quoted by Meeks between brackets is taken from Keynes. And the whole argument is taken from Hollis, who is quoted saying that "there are rational habits and, were there not, we could not talk, plan, associate, build, reason or

confusion about Hume's thinking, because he never said that induction was inconvenient or denied that people use past experience as a practical guide for dealing with the future.[11] He just claimed that induction was not (and cannot be) justified. And its justification is not available yet.

Keynes and his followers in this crusade in favor of induction have not succeeded in showing its possibility. Up to now there is no logic that can be used to identify judgments of partial implication whose validity may be recognized inter-subjectively. In fact, their confidence in the possibility of being successful at reaching this goal is strange given that taking some of their expressions at face value they even have doubts about the possibility of an objective *deductive* logic! How can somebody believe that a "valid" inductive logic may be constructed if at the same time they declare themself a skeptic about the universal and objective validity of the basic axioms of standard logic?

Ultimately, although the vindication of some logic wider than deductive logic has many supporters, it has not been properly elaborated yet and only counts with intuitive appeal. It cannot be used, then, to support the claim that economic agents may behave in a rational way under uncertainty. At best it is only a working hypothesis waiting for further elaboration. More compelling (and better founded in Keynes' economic thinking) is the particular thesis stating that some agents, operating in a particular market (the stock market) may somehow manage to perform a "calculation" on the expected profitability of different investment projects. In this case, GT gives us an accurate description of the steps that have to be taken if investment decisions are to be rational. In the next section I will examine this assertion.

---

perform many other tasks which make social life possible...if the point is missed, large areas of social action are wrongly classed as non-rational" (p. 31). The trick is considering rational all human conduct needed to preserve (or greatly facilitate) social life. With a similar argument Hayek (1992) considers rational the behavior of those people who submit a-critically to those rules and norms needed by the proper working of the market.

[11] By the way, it is not true that one cannot dispense with past experience. Sometimes there is no past experience at all to follow, and there are occasions in which agents choose deliberately a contra inductive procedure. Otherwise there would be no diversity in human behavior, something that in Keynes consideration was essential for economic stability.

4. Rational calculation

In Chapter 11, as well as in some passages of Chapter 12 of his GT, Keynes analyzes the determinants of investment at the aggregate level and states that investment occurs when the marginal efficiency of capital (MEC) is higher than the interest rate. The marginal efficiency of capital is the difference between the offered price of a capital good and its expected profitability. At the microeconomic level Keynes talks as if the investor *could* calculate the probable (future) yields of its present decisions. He seems to believe, indeed, that there are some special people who have the talents for acquiring in the present the knowledge of the future yield to be obtained by an additional unit of capital good.[12] So, regarding investment decisions the probability theory developed in his *Treatise* seems to be valid: starting from the limited evidence available for them, agents can "calculate" (and rank) the probabilities of the different investment projects in which they are interested. More precisely, what the investor could "calculate" is the marginal efficiency of different units of capital (k1, k2, ..., kn) which could be added to his existing capital stock. What is "calculated" and compared then are units like MEk1, MEk2...., etc., where MEkj represents the marginal efficiency of the j unit of capital. The investor chooses the option that tops his ranking (provided that the MEkj selected be higher than the interest rate). The investment decision, then, would not be arbitrary, because it will be supported by the "calculation" alluded. In terms of the *Treatise* it would be the result of a *rational* belief in the superiority of the selected option.

Those who take Keynes's statements literally accept this rationalistic vision of investment decisions. Chick, for instance, claims that "Keynes' theory has two elements: 'rational calculation' (Chapter 11) and animal spirits (...). Rational calculation depends on a comparison of an observable variable, the rate of interest, with the marginal efficiency of capital, comprising firms' long period expectations of profit and the supply price of capital goods" (Chick,

---

[12] Keynes distinguished two quite different types of agents in the stock market. The "ignorants", that is, those "persons who do not manage and have no special knowledge of the circumstances, either actual or prospective, of the business in question", and the "experts" or "professional investors" which are able to make "superior long-term forecasts of the probable yield of an investment over its whole life" (Keynes, 2002, chap. 12).

2002)[13]. A similar understanding underlies Dow's remark that "while Chapter 11 of *The General Theory* analyses the investment decision as a rational comparison between the marginal efficiency of capital (which depends on its prospective yield) and the rate of interest, Chapter 12 delves more deeply into how the prospective yield is arrived at" (Dow, 2003, p. 210). They failed to see any problem in melding both views, and labeled as "dualistic" those positions that, as Shackell's, give up rational calculation and picture agents as being driven only by animal spirits.

Other post-Keynesians seem to share their conviction in agents' capacity to decide rationally. However, neither Chick nor Dow nor, as far as I know, any other author, make it clear the nature of the "calculation" the investor has to do to obtain "values" of the marginal efficiency of the different units of capital he is considering (note, by the way, that the expression "rational calculation" is used between brackets by Chick). They also failed to clarify what it means to "compare" the MEkj chosen with the interest rate and in what sense the decision to invest could be rational in conditions where uncertainty prevails. To show where the problem lies, let's see what is behind such "calculation".

Let k be an additional unit of capital (say a particular machine usable along some period). The decision problem that the entrepreneur faces is to incorporate it to the capital already owned or not to do it. According to Keynes, for this decision it is vital to take into account two factors: the interest rate i and the marginal efficiency of the machine, k, but he clarifies that the latter variable is the vital one in investment decisions. In turn, the key variables that according to GT affect MEk are the *expected* changes in the interest rates, the value of money and the production costs (changes in the wage unit and technological innovations). The expectations that agents form about the future "values" of these three factors will be relevant in deciding if k should be acquired or not. Because the interest rate is known, the decision problem depends entirely on the value of MEk. If its determination were worked out in a completely arbitrary manner, the referred comparison between MEk and i could hardly be considered rational in any

---

[13] Making things worse, Chick says that "the latter variable is problematic because individual firms cannot know the supply price, which will vary with the level of activity".

acceptable sense. Consequently, what the defenders of the rationalist view need to do is to show that MEk can be formed in an acceptable rational way.

It is tempting to think that the agent could use the economic theory for MEk's estimation, but why should agents know the theory? In fact, Keynes offered a revolutionary view, which contradicted conventional wisdom and was, and still is, tremendously resisted and badly understood.[14] Besides, GT refers to *aggregate* economic mechanisms, which only partially affect individual interests. Keep in mind Hayek's argument in *The use of knowledge in society*, where rightly, I think, he claimed that scientific (theoretic) knowledge was of no use for agents involved in production (or, we may add, investment) decisions. Even if agents knew economic theory pretty well, it is unlikely that they would consider changes in those variables that GT identifies as significant for the determination of MEC (aggregate level) to be equally significant for the determination of the marginal efficiency of k (the particular unit of capital goods whose addition to the existing capital they are considering). It is more reasonable then to suppose that agents employ just a few rudiments of the practical economic wisdom closely related to their particular interests. *They do not reason systematically on the basis of economic theory*. They do not count with a "logic" for making profit: a special way of thinking and reason designed to deal with the particular economic events in which they are personally interested. Finally, it is one thing to know generically what are the main factors affecting MEC, and a completely different thing to have a rational procedure for attaching values to them.

---

[14] The difficulties posed by GT to its readers, even the most able among them, may be fully appreciated by the reactions of some economists contemporary to Keynes. "The book, moreover, breaks with traditional modes of approach to its problems at a number of points – at the greatest possible number of points, one suspects – and no old term for an old concept is used when a new one can be coined, and if old terms are used new meanings are generally assigned to them. The definitions provided, moreover, are sometimes of unbelievable complexity. The old-fashioned economist must, therefore, struggle not only with new ideas and new methods of manipulating them, but also with a new language" (Viner, 1995, p. 47). Also Keynes's method was hard to understand at that time: "What is mysterious and difficult to state clearly is the manner in which Mr. Keynes sets up an economics system on the basis of assumptions which imply that these variables or variable-complexes are either fixed or are determined by other forces than the mutual adjustment of supply and demand, i.e., by 'bargains' or public authority, or 'psychology' or some other deus ex machina" (Knight, 1995, pp. 73 - 74).

Rationality

How then do agents manage to "calculate" MEk? Nowhere has Keynes given a description of such procedure. I think he didn't simply because his considerations regarding expectations' formation under uncertainty show there is no way at all to estimate MEk rationally. This in turn deprives of rationality any comparison one would like to make between MEk and the interest rate. Under uncertainty conditions it is not possible to calculate, either with certainty or with known probability.

> "By 'uncertain' knowledge, let me explain, I do not mean merely to distinguish what is known for certain from what is only probable. The game of roulette is not subject, in this sense, to uncertainty; nor is the prospect of a Victory bond being drawn. Or, again, the expectation of life is only slightly uncertain. Even the weather is only moderately uncertain. The sense in which I am using the term is that in which the prospect of an European war is uncertain, or the price of copper and the rate of interest twenty years hence, or the obsolescence of a new invention, or the position of private wealth-owners in the social system in 1970. About these matters there is no scientific basis on which to form any calculable probability whatever. We simply do not know" (Keynes, 1937).

From the fact that someone decides to buy k and that this presupposes he expects to obtain a value (profit) from k greater than the one he would gain assigning that amount of money some other way, one should not conclude he has an objective procedure to set the value of MEk. It is of no use to have a formula which gives you some specific number once precise values are injected into it. The problem lies precisely in the inputs that have to be incorporated.[15] As Mises said these are not data; they are just completely

---

[15] "Writers on Keynes's theory of investment incentive give all their attention to the concepts of the marginal efficiency of capital and the interaction of a quantity so named with the interest-rate on loans of money. To do so is to study the formal configuration of the engine without asking about its thermal source of power. The marginal efficiency of capital is nothing but a formal sum waiting for the insertion of numerical values in place of its algebraic symbols. The essential problem of why at any time the investment flow has the size it has is contained in the question what is the source of these numerical values, by what psychic alchemy is the list of

arbitrary conjectures.[16] Consequently, not being able to calculate in the strict sense, no "calculation" may induce people to invest. As Keynes noticed, it was optimism, the preference for action to inaction and a bit of idealism what all along history has impelled entrepreneurs to risk their capital and invest.[17] This set of attitudes form part of what he labeled animal spirits.[18]

5. Conventions

In GT as well as in his 1937 article Keynes offers another version of the human way for dealing with uncertainty: now he says agents recur to what he labels "a practical theory of the future", composed by a set of "techniques" or conventions which allow us "to behave in a manner which saves our faces as rational, economic men". It seems to be a radical departure from his previous positions. This "theory" involves three basic "techniques":

---

incongruous ingredients chosen and fused into an answer to the unanswerable" (Shackle, 1967, chap. 11).

[16] "The engineer – as far as he attends to the technological side of his job – applies only numerical relations established by the method of the experimental natural sciences; the businessmen cannot avoid numerical terms which are the outcome of his understanding of future human conduct". No matter how precise and accurate a formula can be, never must be forgotten "the uncertainty and speculative character of their items and of all computations based on them" (Mises, 1996, p. 215). These numbers are just arbitrary conjectures about the future conditions that will prevail in the market.

[17] "If human nature felt no temptation to take a chance, no satisfaction (profit apart) in constructing a factory, a railway, a mine or a farm, there might not be much investment merely as a result of cold calculation" (Keynes, 2002, chap. 12, III.).

[18] "... a large proportion of our positive activities depend on spontaneous optimism rather than on a mathematical expectation, whether moral or hedonistic or economic. Most, probably, of our decisions to do something positive, the full consequences of which will be drawn out over many days to come, can only be taken as a result of animal spirits – of a spontaneous urge to action rather than inaction, and not as the outcome of a weighted average of quantitative benefits multiplied by quantitative probabilities". Then, "if the animal spirits are dimmed and the spontaneous optimism falters, leaving us to depend on nothing but a mathematical expectation, enterprise will fade and die". He ends pointing that "individual initiative will only be adequate when reasonable calculation is supplemented and supported by animal spirits, so that the thought of ultimate loss which often overtakes pioneers, as experience undoubtedly tells us and them, is put aside as a healthy man puts aside the expectation of death" (Keynes, 2002, chap. 12, VII).

Rationality

"(1) We assume that the present is a much more serviceable guide to the future than a candid examination of past experience would show it to have been hitherto. In other words we largely ignore the prospect of future changes about the actual character of which we know nothing"

"(2) We assume that the existing state of opinion as expressed in prices and the character of existing output is based on a correct summing up of future prospects, so that we can accept it as such unless and until something new and relevant comes into the picture"

"(3) Knowing that our individual judgment is worthless, we endeavor to fall back on the judgment of the rest of the world which is perhaps better informed. That is, we endeavor to conform with the behavior of the majority or the average. The psychology of a society of individuals each of whom is endeavoring to copy the others leads to what we may strictly term a conventional judgment" (Keynes, 1937).

Here Keynes *says* (or seems to say) that under uncertainty it is possible to decide to follow conventions rationally. Some of his followers share his conviction on this matter. Mizuhara, for instance, states that "this is the best that investors can do under such circumstances, and therefore ... their opting to follow existing conventions is to this extent rational" (Mizuhara, 2003, p. 203). As we saw, however, the Keynesian analysis of investment behavior suggests a different interpretation. As Shackle made clear the central message of GT is that investment behavior is *not* rational[19]. The relevant point, I think, is not to register placidly Keynes's assertions, but to examine critically his claim that following rules or conventions involves rationality. This task has been partially undertaken: techniques (1) and (2) presuppose induction, a point treated above in Section 1, and we will not repeat here

---

[19] "Chapter 11 shows us the arithmetic of the marginal efficiency of capital and its relation with interest-rates, a matter for actuaries and slide-rules. Chapter 12 reveals the hollowness of all this. The material for the slide-rules is absent, or arbitrary. Investment is an *irrational* activity, or a non-rational one" (Shackle, 1967, cap. 11, on line).

what has been already said. More interesting, and actually hotly debated, is the case of imitative behavior mentioned by Keynes in (3). In what sense can it be rational to imitate other people?[20]

The rationality of mimic behavior under uncertainty has been defended by Dupuy: "(if) I know nothing about the social context in which I find myself (as in the context of a panic), there is some chance that others may know something, and by imitating them, I may draw some advantage from their knowledge" (quoted in Bibow et. al., 2003, p. 191). This view has some flaws. First, the analogy with panic is unfortunate, because even if it were true that under panic one's reaction were to follow other people, this is not the kind of reaction we generally consider properly thoughtful. So, although people might adopt mimic responses in cases like these I fail to see why such behavior should be considered rational. Even worse, Dupuy's argument supposes a certain vision of the agents (as well as the environment in which they decide) which is not compatible with a situation that most post-Keynesians (following Keynes) call fundamental uncertainty. If agents know or believe the circumstances that in the future will validate or invalidate their actual decisions do not exist yet, they cannot reason in the way Dupuy pretends. How may I believe that my neighbors know better than I what the future will be like if at the same time I believe that an essential component in the determination of the future is not available at present (and cannot be available yet)? Dupuys's argument works only if it is assumed that agents believe that the knowledge required for guessing the future is already available in advance. So, even if they do not have such knowledge other people could have it (and it would be a good strategy to copy them).[21] To the extent that I think this is a false and unreasonable view, the "rationality" that could be attributed to agents who have such an idea of knowledge should be merely a coherentist one: mimicry would be rational relative to their beliefs (which are not only false but also completely unsound, except from a deterministic metaphysics currently completely discredited). This weak rationality may well be attributed to consumers' horoscopes, but not to economic agents: in this case something stronger and more substantial is required. The coherentist rationality which merely asserts the logical

---

[20] This topic was approached from another perspective on Chapter 4.
[21] In Chapter 4 this scenario is designed as *complex* (in a sense that is quite different from uncertainty).

compatibility of agents' beliefs and decisions (without judging the true value of their beliefs) is again the weak rationality of mainstream theory.

In Gillies (2003) we find a different view about the manner in which expectations are formed. According to him given severe uncertainty "entrepreneurs imitate each other so that the group comes to have more or less the same expectation" (p. 124). But, as he recognizes, even if this were the way in which conventional wisdom is formed, in itself it says nothing about its rationality. He remarks, in fact, that Keynes himself was a skeptic on this point.[22] However he thinks there is a roundabout way of defending mimics' rationality: a theorem of probability theory shows that in betting against another person or group, each member of a given group profits from sharing a common betting quotient. Gillies' argument is essentially the same as the second one advanced by Meeks. Meeks defended the rationality of performing induction arguing that if "technique" X (say induction) is necessary to obtain Y (which is desirable or even badly needed), performing X cannot be considered irrational or not rational. I find his argument persuasive, but I think he is wrong. Performing X may be considered rational *only if* the agent wants Y, is quite conscious of the relationship between X and Y, and it is precisely this knowledge which gives him a reason to perform X. In deciding on the rationality of following conventions both things are required: good reasons to behave this way and awareness of such reasons on the part of the individual. In the present case *he* (not Gillies) must know that imitating other people is better for him than not do it, and this knowledge has to be the reason for behaving the way he does.

In Gillies' account nothing suggests that in the process of convergence to a shared betting quotient the individuals are driven by the reasons advanced by Gillies in favor of such behavior. The shared betting quotient is not a consciously performed strategy pursued by each member of the group. They are completely unaware of the reasons given by Gillies in favor of imitating one another. Supposing it is permissible to talk of rationality in cases like these, its only foundation seems to be that they are successful.

---

[22] "Keynes's point is that because of a lack of information and because of the general uncertainty of the future, entrepreneurs cannot form a rational expectation, which then determines their investment decisions" (Gillies, 2003, p. 124).

In the first two sections we explained the nature of the "calculation" performed under uncertainty and gave the reasons that prevented us from considering it rational. It is worth noting that in an important sense imitative behavior/mimicry is even less substantiated than the "calculation". To see why it may be useful to pay attention to the nature of the judgments involved in each case. The probability judgments of TP are subjective in the sense that each individual makes an estimation of the degree of partial entailment between *e* and *h*, without any reference to the judgments of other people[23]. On the contrary, judgments resulting from imitation are deprived of personal critical examination of the available evidence and its relationship with the resultant hypothesis. They merely consist in the appropriation of the opinion of other people.[24] While the "calculation" relies on our own estimation of how strong the degree of support that *e* gives to *h* is; in the judgments arrived at by mimic behavior this estimation is absent. They are based on a mechanical reaction to follow the crowd. A case by case analysis is not necessary here. The copycat follows just one and the same rule: keep yourself as close as possible to the general opinion at all times.

Finally, there is a general argument against the supposed rationality of imitative behavior under uncertainty: if it were rational to copy other people, those who do not behave in this way (the ones who are dissenters regarding

---

[23] "According to Keynes, the individual has to consider each case on its own merits and by a personal autonomous judgement independent of traditional judgement, that is, independent of the judgement of the majority or of the most common opinion" (Carabelli, 2003, p. 226). This is in fact the view developed by Keynes in his Treatise on Probability. Carabelli rewords slightly the following passage of *My Early Beliefs*: "We claimed the right to judge every individual case on its merits, and the wisdom, experience and self-control to do so successfully" (quoted in Davis, 2003, p. 106)

[24] Keynes' anti conventionalist stance may be defended by looking at his personal history. According to Hayek, "John Maynard Keynes, (is) one of the most representative intellectual leaders of a generation emancipated from traditional morals. Keynes believed that, by taking account of foreseeable effects, he could build a better world than by submitting to traditional abstract rules. Keynes used the phrase 'conventional wisdom' as a favorite expression of scorn, and in a revealing autobiographical account ... he told how the Cambridge circle of his younger years, most of whose members later belonged to the Bloomsbury Group, 'entirely repudiated a personal liability on us to obey general rules' and how they were 'in the strict sense of the term, inmoralists'" (Hayek, 1992, p. 57). Although it cannot be doubted that in Keynes's concern conventions were the basis upon which expectations were formed, the claim that he also found this commitment with conventions rational is unfounded. This view is Hayek's, not Keynes'.

conventional wisdom) should be labeled as irrational (or not rational) people. The trouble is that Keynes himself thought in a different way: he never disqualified the diversity of reactions. Whoever thinks he knows better than the market may be perfectly right. Applied to behavior, the terms rational and not rational have no clear meaning under uncertainty. It is impossible to recognize in advance which kind of action is rational and which is a "deviation" from the right behavior. Besides, sometimes Keynes seemed to be very critical of conventional wisdom, which became more and more dominated by the opinions of the less able agents. A solid defense of the rationality of imitative behavior consistent with his views on investment decisions and the workings of the stock market is still lacking. But, if I am not mistaken, this defense may prove to be highly implausible.

Chapter 7
Testing and learning

Testing and making experiments is a useful and legitimate activity in science and experimental economics is an expanding branch of economic theory. In spite of the interest and resources this activity attracts, experimental economics faces serious difficulties. A good part of the current debate about experimentation in economics concerns its external validity. In this section, that assumes radical uncertainty, the decisive thing is to examine what meaning could the accomplishment of a test in a time t0 have if the theory or model that is tested makes reference to events that will happen at a later time t1.

Consider two kinds of choices: between hypothesis and between actions (decisions). First we are going to examine the case of choices between alternatives under conditions of certainty.

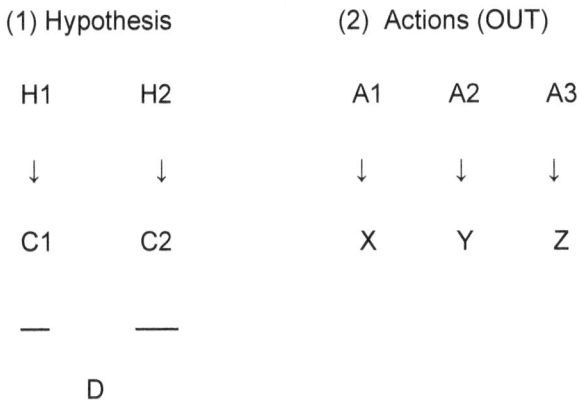

(1) Hypothesis		(2) Actions (OUT)		
H1	H2	A1	A2	A3
↓	↓	↓	↓	↓
C1	C2	X	Y	Z
—	—			
	D			

It is worth taking note of some key differences between (1) and (2).

Schema (1) represents the traditional test between rival conjectures, H1 and H2. The respective consequences C1 and C2 are deduced from the premises and then contrasted against a set D of relevant data. If C1 (but not C2) is contradicted by the available evidence H2 will be preferred. Schema (2) represents choices according to Ordinal Utility Theory (OUT). Given a set of three goods, X, Y and Z, rational agents can form a complete and transitive rank of preferences among them. Suppose an agent prefers Y to X and X to Z. A1 ↓ X represents the action of choosing X, A2 ↓ Y choosing Y and A3 ↓ Z choosing Z. Given his preferences the agent will pick up action A1. He will do it because the consequence of this action is preferable to the consequences of any of the other available alternative actions. There are two basic differences among these kinds of choices.

1) When hypotheses are evaluated, the preferences regarding their consequences do not matter. It may be that a subject prefers that the world was as it is asserted by H1 − not as H2 says it is, but this is irrelevant. This type of discrimination between consequences, according to their relevance for the interests of particular individuals, is precisely what has been reproached to Friedman. The reproach is reasonable as far as the interest that a subject has in the consequences of a given hypothesis is completely irrelevant from the strictly semantic or epistemic point of view that only has to do with the truth-status of the hypothesis given all the relevant available evidence.

2) The choice between rival hypotheses does not take place at the same moment at which the consequences are identified (that is to say, before being confronted with the data). The decision is taken ex-post, once the relevant evidence has been gathered and compared with the consequences in order to establish their truth-value. The choice between actions (i.e., taking decisions), however, is made *before* (and *independently of*) the experimentation (test) of the consequences, and on the base of the utility that they have for the decision-maker. The choice between rival hypotheses is made by paying attention to the truth-value of their consequences. The choice between rival actions is made by the utility that their consequences will presumably offer to the decision-maker. In the

first case, the rational chooser takes into account the empirical test. In the second case, this step is omitted: the rationality involved in carrying out A2 does not require later empirical confirmation. Choices between hypotheses are ex-post; choices between decisions (actions) are ex-ante.

OUT is a notion of rationality that suitably fits the choice-situation in which certainty governs. In these conditions the subject knows (trivially) the consequences of his actions and the utility that each of them will yield. It is another way of saying that he knows his utility function. Therefore, it is not necessary to verify whether the utility expected from the chosen good at the moment t0 in which it was chosen, is indeed so at a later moment t1 in which the chosen option is consumated. Agents do not need to verify whether their utility function is correct or not: the empirical step (test), that is necessary in (1), is not necessary in (2), because the assumption of "certainty" provides the knowledge that testing is supposed to provide.

Boland has challenged this interpretation. Following Popper he considers that agents' preferences are hypotheses, which means that an agent *believes* (ex-ante) that he prefers Y to X, and X to Z. He believes that his own utility–function is like the one represented by the ranking

Y

X

Z

In this interpretation the subject is "uncertain" in a different way: à la Popper. To show the difference we have established between *knowing* (with certainty) and *believing* (to consider that knowledge itself fallible)[1]. If the subject knows he is fallible, he must admit that his ex-ante beliefs about his preferences could be falsified ex-post. It would be necessary then to distinguish between "utility 1" (ex-ante) and a different "utility 2" (ex-post).

---

[1] Boland would probably reject this distinction. He considers that knowledge is *conjectural* knowledge and that knowledge is *objective*. Beliefs instead are psychological states.

The first is the one which is "expected" and the second the one which is verified. This last sort of utility is the one that an individual will experience once the result of his action has been finally realized.

Once choices are treated as hypotheses, Boland can introduce the notion of rationality of Popperian epistemology within economic theory: to be rational is to critically examine the hypotheses that one holds. The rationality of an agent lies in his disposition to rigorously contrast his initial hypotheses about his preferences. The rationality of the subject does not come from his initial choice according to the "utility 1" that the options report to him, but in the process of adjustment of these beliefs according to the habitual mechanism of conjectures and refutations. To be rational is to have a *critical attitude*. Boland replaces the traditional notion of rationality in economics which is defined in terms of preferences, by a notion that links rationality with procedures that put previous beliefs under empirical control.

Actually, from this perspective one could distinguish between a weak rationality (that identifies a rational decision with the ex-ante belief that the chosen course of action will result in greater satisfaction to the decision-maker (it has greater "utility 1" for him). And a strong rationality, that demands that the subject corroborates whether his original presumption is or not verified (and not by means of any procedure, but by putting under test his initial conjectures). This opens the possibility that the subject may try to falsify his initial presumption that he does prefer Y to X. He can do it in a second step by choosing X, and comparing which of both results is more satisfying to him. This way he could corroborate his previous hypothesis or refute it. In this last case he will remake his utility-function.

This "critical rationality" (founded on Popper's view) emphasizes the insufficiency of a merely coherentist approach to rationality and the necessity to incorporate empirical evidence to the analysis of rational decisions. But it can also be applied to risky situations (choices between lotteries). Let us see now the scheme (3) that represents decisions under risky conditions (or "uncertainty", in the mainstream sense of the term).

(3) Actions (EUT)

A1	A2	A1	A2
S1	S1	S2	S2
↓	↓	↓	↓
C11	C12	C21	C22

Here A1 and A2 are the available actions and S1 and S2 represent hypotheses about the actual states of the world. C11 is the consequence that the individual will obtain by doing A1 if the world is like S1. And so on. We have two types of hypothesis: those that refer to actions and those that refer to states. If the agent has time (his decision needn't be taken right away) before deciding what action to undertake he can make some experiments to determine which of the alternative states is the one that may prevail. This would start up a process of test and error. But this procedure cannot be used without restrictions, because the successful test could ultimately completely eliminate uncertainty changing the nature of the choice problem. The example of the sixth egg of Savage's illustrates this situation. What characterizes (defines) "uncertainty" in Savage's sense is that in the moment of deciding the subject *knows* which the possible states of the world are, but he does *not* know which of them is actually effective.

The interesting thing about decisions under *uncertainty* in the conventional way is that testing does not play any relevant role (when it does, uncertainty disappears and the choice problem becomes completely different from the initial one). As the test does not serve to say for sure what the actual state of the world is, the subject cannot but assign subjective probabilities to states S1 and S2.

In fact, in schema (3) only one of the two possible worlds is actually given, although which is which is not known. And the consequences only depend on the *actual* state of the world and the selected action. But if one considers choices in conditions of *radical uncertainty* a reference to *future* states must be incorporated. The problem of choice under these circumstances can be represented thus:

(4) Actions (EUT)

A1	A2	A1	A2
S1	S1	S2	S2

St1	St1	St1	St1
St2	St2	St2	St2
....			
....			
Stn	Stn	Stn	Stn
↓	↓	↓	↓
C11	C12	C21	C22

The actions and the states of the world that are represented above the solid line of the scheme are the ones that govern the present moment t0. The subject considers that the consequences of his present action depend jointly on this very action, the actual state of the world and the events that are going to occur in the forthcoming lapse t0 – tn. He does not know the states t1 – tn, but if he decides to collect new data he could find out something about the present t0. If his search were completely satisfactory he could find out how the actual state "really" is in t0 (and in that case the uncertainty about it would disappear).

If he prolongs his search of information, some of the states that were future in t0 will update, which does not prevent him from continuing to be uncertain about them (something that could prompt him to gather new information over and over again). But his decision must be taken at some point, and whenever it is made there will always be future states of the world about which information cannot be gathered simply because they are not available yet. What believers in induction hope is that inductive inferences could transform the available evidence – relevant to considering the present state of the world – into relevant evidence about the future states of the world.

They are wrong. The incorporation of new information makes sense only if the future is to be similar to the past. Any kind of empirical test, whatever form it adopts, will not make sense, however, if the world is *uncertain* because in such a world induction does not work (this is Davidson's thesis about the ergodic assumption). Past experience is not a useful guide to guess the future in these conditions (it only serves when the future, somehow, is already implicit in the present). Since some may find these assertions too strong it is convenient to clear some things up. Consider a situation in which the three following hypothesis are tested in the methodological traditional sense:

H1: Metals dilate when they are warmed up;

H2: In the lapse between the present moment and the twelve following months, metals will dilate when they are warmed up;

H3: In the course of the 23rd century metals will dilate when they are warmed up.

In principle H1 and H2 can be tested without difficulty: all of the relevant experiments made in the course of a year will serve to the effect. The problem is how to contrast H3. Or, more clearly stated, how can we take advantage of the past experimental results (or of those that will be made in the period between the present moment and the end of the 23rd century) to decide something about the truth of H3? I believe the only way to use past experience is to assume that the world is *repetitive*. In a non-repetitive world in which relevant novelties unexpectedly arise testing is irrelevant. Popper has emphasized that there is a *logical* problem involved in taking advantage of *favorable* experience. It could be said that to use any sort of experience (favorable or not) with the purpose of assessing hypotheses concerning the future involves also an *ontological* problem if the world is *non* repetitive.[2]

These considerations are applicable to decisions in conditions of radical uncertainty. If the actions that I undertake in t0 will have very different consequences according to the eventual state of the world in t1, it is crucial

---

[2] In a non-repetitive world testing has no purpose. This is also valid for the natural world, so nothing is said here about the consciousness that agents may have of the non-repetitive nature of social processes and the particular limitations that this fact imposes on their knowledge. These issues will be approached in Chapter 8.

to gather reliable knowledge about these states. But how could I evaluate in t0 my beliefs about the state of the world in t1? If the world were repetitive (governed by immutable laws) and these laws were known, I could assume that what I find out about the present state is relevant to determine how the future state (the one that will prevail) will be. It would make then sense to apply a strategy for gathering empirical evidence (a sequence of actions to collect new data). But if the world is not repetitive, what makes me think that the new information may be at all useful regarding future events?

2. Learning

The idea that agents can learn has a central place in economics. It seems easy to defend it. Nobody questions that learning is possible and appropriate institutions for achieving it do exist. Nevertheless, the contexts in which one can claim that economic agents learn are very special. Under certainty, they have already learned by hypothesis. In conditions of risk, however, learning is somewhat more problematic.

During the second half of the 20th century as well as in recent years a good number of experiments designed to test EUT have shown the recurrent presence of anomalies in peoples' behavior. A frequent standard argument against the relevance of anomalous behavior is that agents *can learn*[3]. Since errors are costly – the argument goes – people will learn and correct their choices in such a way that biases will be gradually eliminated. Is it true that given risky conditions agents can learn from their mistakes and correct them? A moderate answer is "not always". Tversky (1974) as well as Tversky and Kahneman (1974), show that under uncertainty individuals make systematic mistakes in the formation of their probability judgments. The important point is that subjects keep behaving in a wrong way after being informed of the errors committed and instructed how to cope with

---

[3] Other arguments for rejecting the so-called anomalies are these: (a) anomalies have been obtained in ill-designed circumstances characterized by insufficient incentives; (b) given that individual deviations are *random* they will cancel each other at the aggregate level, and (c) it has been held (Friedman, 1953) that market mechanisms (arbitrage and competition) work in the right direction, eliminating the influence (and in the long run the very presence in the market) of those agents who behave in a sub-optimal way.

them. Einhorn and Hogarth (1978) argued in a similar way. It seems that learning isn't an easy task at all, and only takes place when relatively exceptional conditions are fulfilled.

> "The problem with many economic models of learning is that they seem to apply to a very static environment. In fact, such models seem to be directly applicable only to the situation in which Bill Murray finds himself in the movie *Ground Hog Day*. In the movie, Bill Murray is a TV weatherman sent to report on whether the groundhog sees his shadow on Feb. 2. Murray's character ends up reliving the same day over and over again. Although he is a slow learner, the opportunity to rerun the same day repeatedly, and to learn from the consequences of his actions each time, creates a controlled experiment in which he is able to learn many things eventually, from how to prevent accidents to how to play the piano. Alas, life is not like *Ground Hog Day*. In life, each day is different, and the most important of life's decisions, such as choosing a career or spouse, offer only a few chances for learning!" (Thaler, 1986, pp. 135-136).[4]

If it is true, as Prospect Theory asserts, that given risky contexts agents suffer different kinds of "cognitive illusions" that generate insurmountable deviations from rational decision-making (the so called "effects"), the more difficult it will be to learn in an environment of radical uncertainty.

It is worth then exploring more thoroughly what type of things we can learn in these much more demanding conditions. Ordinary experience and common sense can serve as a base for approaching this question. We can learn – to register and to organize – any of the available data. And we can update this information as new pieces of evidence become available. Everything that can be learned is almost "behind" ours in the line of time (and only a small portion of events are actually present to us). Measurements, tests,

---

[4] Tversky and Kahneman (1986, pp. S274.S275) offer a more accurate classification of the many circumstances in which learning could not take place.

experiments, are forms for collecting or organizing information already available.

Is there anything else that can be learned (in addition to mathematics and logic that we did not examine here)? Could causal connections between events, factual laws and mechanisms be learned (discovered)? Some invariant principles perhaps? Can we know something of this sort? Can invariant regularities under certain special conditions be known? For example, can the fact that an event A appears next to event B in conditions N be learned? If we knew this, then generating N (in any other place or time) and producing A we would obtain B. This is the idea that is behind the concepts of nomological machine or mechanism. The future can be constructed so that certain regularities emerge. This would eliminate uncertainty at the cost of transforming the world into an extension of the laboratory. Successful experimentation shows that we are able to learn the conditions in which different types of events are regularly connected.

But conceiving economic processes like sequences of events in which uncertainty reigns, where consequently there are "no laws", nor "invariants" or "mechanisms" to discover, the kind of learning that experiments or last experience provide is of no use for the future, because it eliminates innovation and creativity and does not take into account the arboreal character and the open-ended nature of the economic process that was described at length in Chapter Five. However, as said before, we can gather precise information, restricted in space and time (data). But, what is the purpose of obtaining this sort of information if uncertainty about future events prevails? Here we meet once again the problem we talked about when testing was analyzed (in fact testing is an aspect of the strategy of learning). As we saw, the problem is that taking uncertainty seriously puts in question the relevance the data obtained by means of testing or experimentation has for future situations.

Let us illustrate this point by means of an application of Bayes' rule, one of the main ways for updating information (that is, learning). I claim that it is a logical resource that only has practical relevance in what later – in Chapter Eight – will be called *complex* (as different from *uncertain*) situations. (* This example was taken from the Stanford Encyclopedia of Philosophy.)

Testing and learning

An individual asks for the probability that JD (a North American citizen that was alive at the beginning of 2000) passed away in the course of that year. As he finds out that in that period the American total population amounts to 275 million, of which 2.4 million died, the probability that he looks for is given by the rate of global mortality.

$$P(H) = (2,4)/(275) = 0,000872$$

This is an objective probability, in the sense that it is calculated based on common usage data (anyone facing a similar problem would use the same data in the same way). But suppose that later the individual receives new information: JD was a senior citizen – older than 75 at the beginning of 2000. This information is also objective, in the previous sense. The important thing is that on the base of this new data he can update his initial estimation. It is necessary now to recalculate the probability of H in light of the new evidence S:

$$P(H/S)$$

Now the rate of global mortality no longer matters and can be discarded. What really matters in the new situation is to find out the rate of mortality among the people that is 75 or older. Looking again at the official statistics the subject finds out that in year 2000 there were 16.6 million seniors in that situation, of which 1.36 million died. The updated probability of H is now

$$P(H) = P(H/S) = (1,36)/(16,6) = 0,082$$

In this example the subject considers the probability of an event that has already happened and about which the totality of the relevant information is available. As far as new relevant information can be found, the previous estimations can be corrected. And provided that it is *objective* information (we assumed that it is) no discrepancies arise about how to interpret it. In addition the information is expressed in unequivocal quantitative terms.[5]

---

[5] The role of the new coming information is to move the attention from the set of events that were the point of departure towards a sub-dominion of those events. Each new round of information restricts the previous dominion of relevant events (providing precise and noncontroversial information).

Bayes' rule provides a procedure that allows us to use the new information to correct the initial hypothesis. The possibility of learning is unquestionable in this scenario.

By incorporating new information Bayes' theorem transforms the previous degrees of belief, but it does not show that the evidence available now is also relevant for future states. It does not provide information about this. The problem, then, is how the relation of relevance between evidence and hypothesis can be supported when the evidence refers to the past and the present and the hypothesis to the future. Or put in another way, how can the available evidence be relevant if it carries information about states of things (events) that fall outside the dominion of reference of the hypothesis? Relevance can only be predicated assuming an immutable and repetitive ontology. Another way is to maintain that it is possible to learn "laws" or mechanisms or some type of stable sequence that may provide us with a ticket for using the present experience in the estimation of future events. These epistemological vehicles would allow us to use past experience to face the future. But by hypothesis under uncertainty there is no such thing. Therefore one cannot learn stable sequences that keep operating in the future in the same way they do today.

Curiously those who maintain that uncertainty prevails in economic affairs do not reject the ability for learning (Syll, Dow). They do so, it seems to me, because they do not surrender the rationality concept (and rationality and learning come in the same package). It sounds paradoxical to maintain that there exist rational agents without capacity or possibility to learn.

Chapter 8

Six core assumptions for reorienting economics and mainstream philosophy of economics

Introduction

This chapter presents an outline of a theory of economic behavior under uncertainty of three different types of economic agencies: agents, theorists and philosophers, together with the analysis of the practice of agents in their twofold role as *decision-makers* and *lobbyists*. Though ontological issues are at the bottom of our analysis, how the world really is matters less to explaining agents' decisions than the *beliefs* these agents hold about this point.[1] The facts (the prevailing ontology) are more relevant for understanding the *results* of their decisions than their decisions themselves. Therefore, in order to consider agents' behavior it is important to clarify their *beliefs* about both the world they inhabit and the knowledge they have about it. Actually, the agents' behavior will be different if they believe the world is complex or uncertain. If they believe the former and behave rationally, they will seek to use the best available information and to enlarge it as much as possible, in order to improve their decisions.

If they believe that the world is truly uncertain, however, their behavior will be very different. In conditions of risk agents can behave in an ex-ante rational way taking rationality in a subjectivist and coherentist sense. They can do it because they choose between lotteries and they know something relevant about them (their prizes and their associated probabilities). Radical

---

[1] Of course, what has been said does not contradict our thesis that ontology has gnoseological precedence over epistemology. We argued at length that economic processes are ridden by interventions, uncertainty and conflict of interest, and smart (not autistic) agents, theorists and philosophers know this. Once these facts are acknowledged, we can go ahead and start directly with individual and groups' beliefs.

uncertainty means that they do not know that. Now the evidence at hand does not provide them with such information. On the contrary, their ontological and epistemic beliefs should be considered as a key part of the available evidence. The parents playing Lego with their children know the creative nature of the ongoing process and the limits that this situation imposes on the knowledge they could possibly have of it. Their ontological and epistemic beliefs are central elements of their uncertainty. If this reasoning is right, agents cannot behave rationally even if rationality is understood in a weaker subjectivist and coherentist sense, because they are conscious that the "numbers" that any calculation about potential future gains may yield deserve no confidence whatsoever. Their philosophical convictions show them that no ex-ante rational decision is available under true uncertainty. What sort of behavior would be "rational" then? My answer is that provided economics cannot surrender rational terminology, being rational is to intervene *a posteriori* of the original decisions for the purpose of validating them. Agents who believe in the uncertain nature of the world are driven (pushed) to become lobbyists and this contributes to generate open-ended and intervenible economic processes.

What about theorists' behavior? If *theorists* believe, like agents do, that the scenario is uncertain, they should also behave consistently with this belief and their theoretical practice would have to take into account the special nature of economic processes under uncertainty. In particular, they should pay attention to the lobbying practice of agents and to those conditions that enable open-ended and intervenible processes. Besides, if the purpose of economic theory were to render account of the behavior of subjects that know (or think they know) they suffer uncertainty, their theoretical practice should assume that agents behave consistently both with respect to their set of preferences and expectations (which is the usual requirement) *and* regarding their *epistemological and ontological beliefs*. Agents should be represented behaving consistently with respect to *all* their beliefs.

However, conventional theoretical practice is not concerned with uncertain scenarios. Conventional economics chooses to represent *imaginary* worlds which Sugden designated as "parallel" worlds. They belong to the "model world" (as opposed to the real world) and are governed by regularities or invariant conditions. This practice does not necessarily reveal inconsistency, but shows that its subject is the realm of economic representations, not real economies. There are then two forms of theoretical practice in economics: intellectual exercises and feasible sequences of economic events. Each of them is committed to a set of ontological and epistemological assumptions, which will be analyzed in the next pages.

This chapter also contributes to a better understanding of standard epistemology and philosophy of economics, which focuses on economic representations (in particular, models) and assumes a *naturalized* view of science. One of the main goals of mainstream philosophy of economics is to display the rationale of theoretical economics. This orientation is usually referred to as "recovering the practice" of economic theory,[2] and presupposes a commitment to mainstream ontology (i.e., the dismissal of uncertainty, social conflict, innovation and lobbying). If it is true, as some philosophers say (see Morgan, 2012), that many economists see the world only through the lenses of their models, it is clear why so many of the crucial features of economic processes are overlooked in their considerations, both for bookish economics and mainstream philosophy of economics. Indeed, if the philosophers' object of thought were real economic processes they should critically examine the usual ontological and epistemological assumptions of conventional modeling practice; and they should be engaged in developing alternative assumptions for that practice consistent with the presence of uncertainty and with the acceptance of its existence by agents and theorists.

1. Two roles for economic agents

To start, a terminology clarification is advisable. We call individuals (basically consumers and producers) as well as firms (both small and mega-corporations) *economic agents*. As already explained, agents usually face an uncertain scenario of the ontological type. We say that a scenario is complex when all the relevant causal factors that determine the behavior of a phenomenon are present, but agents only know (and combine) *some* of them. Under radical uncertainty, instead, the forthcoming results of the

---

[2] See Caldwell (1994).

agents' current decisions will be also determined by the values that some economic variables will adopt in the future. In an uncertain scenario these future values are unknown because they do not yet exist (actually in the present they are *in principle unknowable*). Under these conditions agents play two different roles along the economic process:

Decision-makers

Lobbyists

Individuals or firms may make economic decisions (behaving as decision-makers), or may influence economic performance in a broader sense with the purpose of enforcing the success of their decisions. In this second role they behave as lobbyists. The category of lobbyists includes the government, communication media, corporations, unions, political parties and any individual or groups of individuals that are strong enough to influence the course of economic events. They may try to influence the expectations of other agents or the relevant economic context (promoting changes into the legislation, new regulations and institutions, etc.).

The distinction between decision-makers and lobbyists refers exclusively to two different roles that the very same agents can play. One way to visualize this difference is to base it at two stages of economic processes: the time before and after decision-making.

t0 (PTF - contracts)   t1   (Lobbying)

.... D ....

Between t0 and t1, agents consider the available alternatives given the information they have, and finally take a decision D. Although decision-makers believe that the world is uncertain they manage to face the situation using PTF[3]. All agents behave in this way in ordinary circumstances. But look what happens then. Many have no choice but to sit down once they

---

[3] According to Keynes, such techniques allow us "to behave in a manner which saves our faces as rational, economic men" (Keynes, 2002, p. 114).

have made a decision and wait to find out what outcome the market will provide for them. But many agents have another option: they can actively intervene in the market after t1, trying to shape the course of economic processes in a way that favors their interests. Lobbyists have behaved as simple decision-makers prior to t1 (i.e., they have naively used PTF), but because they believe that the world is uncertain and have the ability to intervene and help to generate the consequences they want to attain, they take an active participation on the market after t1. Lobbyists may be characterized by three main features:

> 1. Knowledge (beliefs). They believe that the social world is uncertain, that agents decide on the basis of expectations that may be influenced in various ways, using a wide range of information that goes beyond purely economic factors, that institutions and regulations can be made and unmade, etc.

> 2. Consistency. They have a consistent set of beliefs and behave consistently with respect to them.

> 3. Lobbying capacity. Due to the size of their capital or their privileged access to positions of power, they have the strength to intervene effectively on the decisions of other agents, either directly (suggesting to them what to expect), or indirectly (modifying or helping to create the economically relevant context).

Like agents, lobbyists suffer uncertainty too. They are unsure about whether their extra-economic activities (as lobbyists) will allow them to get in the future the results expected in the present. They do not know whether their intervention will be successful given that there are also other lobbyists intervening in order to push the process along lines that are not beneficial for them (remember the Lego-game described in Chapter Four!). Nonetheless they do have some useful knowledge, which encourages them to keep trying to influence the process. For instance, they know what measures (bills, regulations, decision-makers' reactions) will be beneficial for them and the sort of participation that will contribute to enforce those measures and reactions.

2. Theorists

So far we have only referred to agents in their twofold role of *decision makers* and *lobbyists*. Outside the market process but interested in figuring out its workings by building models are the theorists, who have to make their own decisions about whether lobbyists should be included or not, how to depict the relevant agents, what beliefs and expectations should be ascribed to them and how to characterize the economic processes in which agents get involved[4]. What features does their theoretical practice show?

Conventional theoretical practice

From the very beginning, the construction of economic theory as a scientific discipline deliberately assumed a sharp break with the main features that characterize real economies. Mill, Menger, Walras and many other classical economists have stated explicitly from the very beginning that the results of economic science are dissociated from their applications. Lucas has been even more explicit about this issue and recognized that denying uncertainty is a condition for economics to be scientific (Lucas, 1981).[5] As a result, theoretical economic practice has proceeded to make up imaginary worlds inhabited by truly rational agents, where regularities governed by calculable risk can be found, and has focused on the examination of the properties of these representations.

---

[4] Although theorists qua theorists do not actively participate in the economic processes, their theoretical contributions also play an influential role in shaping agents' expectations and hence upon the conformation of the resulting economic phenomena. For this reason they may be considered a particular type of players. Some of them may be lobbyists as long as they represent some particular economic interests, but probably most economists do not intend to perform this role.

[5] "[This hypothesis] will most likely be useful in situations in which the probabilities of interest concern a fairly well defined recurrent event, situations of 'risk' [where] behavior may be explainable in terms of economic theory ... In cases of uncertainty, economic reasoning will be of no value ... Insofar as business cycles can be viewed as repeated instances of essentially similar events, it will be reasonable to treat agents as reacting to cyclical changes as 'risk', or to assume their expectations are rational, that they have fairly stable arrangements for collecting and processing information, and that they utilize this information in forecasting the future in a stable way, free of systemic and easily correctable biases." (Lucas 1981, p. 224) *Studies in Business-Cycle Theory*.

A common way to get models that exclude uncertainty is to adopt what Davidson called the ergodic axiom, which allows one to use past data for assigning probabilities to future phenomena. This axiom is particularly suitable for theoretical practice upon some kinds of imaginary worlds. It presupposes a set of ontological and epistemological assumptions that underlie conventional theoretical practice in economics. It is illuminating to see this set of assumptions as a sophisticated version of Keynes' Practical Theory about the Future (PTF), which allows a scientistic treatment of economic phenomena.[6] Particularly, it allows economists to deal with uncertainty in their theoretical practice. Adapting Keynes' words we will call this set of beliefs Scientific Theory about the Future (STF). Its main presuppositions are:

> 1) Specific economies "contain" laws, mechanisms or some kind of regularities. They are invariant (stable) features of the economic processes that lie below the surface of economic phenomena.

> 2) The role of theoretical practice (or one of its fundamental roles) is to discover these invariants.

> 3) This invariant knowledge refers to the future and is obtainable ex-ante (mainly by models).

To these ontological and epistemological assumptions conventional economics usually adds a practical one:

> 4) Without having the invariant knowledge mentioned in (2) and (3) it is not legitimate to recommend economic policies.

Those theorists who share this set of beliefs model no uncertain contexts and try to describe the behavior of a mechanism that generates a stable process from the interplay of agents, regardless the deliberate attempts of

---

[6] "Paul Samuelson [1969] has written that if economists hope to move economics from 'the realm of history' into 'the realm of science' they must impose the 'ergodic hypothesis' on their theory. In other words Nobel Prize Winner Paul Samuelson has made the ergodic axiom the *sine qua non* for the scientific method in economics. Lucas and Sargent [1981] have also claimed the principle behind the ergodic axiom is the only scientific method of doing economics" (Davidson, 2012, p. 59).

the State to interfere with the "natural" course of events. From this perspective it is natural to stress that the role of social or economic theory is to investigate the unwanted (and unexpected) consequences of agents' decisions. And it is also clear why those theorists need not consider incorporating lobbyists to their approach. The lobbying activity has no place when agents are able to take ex-ante rational decisions. The only case in which the lobbyists' role is taken into account concerns the participation of the State, which is usually incorporated in combination with the view that its interventions will always be a failure.

Summing up, conventional theoretical practice has not considered those central features that characterize economies as uncertain systems. Rather it has proceeded in two steps: a) creating imaginary worlds governed by regularities or invariant parameters that do not have a counterpart in real economies; b) exploring the workings of these imaginary worlds. I suggest that such theoretical practice has developed in an inward-looking way (focusing more on its own product than paying attention to economic phenomena as they occur in specific concrete economies). Conventional economics has created its own object of study. Substituting the analysis of real economies for the examination of imaginary worlds saves theorists from falling into inconsistencies: their belief in the uncertain nature of current economic processes is not inconsistent with their belief that within the model-world regular knowledge of "future" events is possible (where "future" refers to logical, not historical, time).

Alternative theoretical practice

Describing agents' behavior, I assumed that they were aware they were facing an uncertain context. With more reason, theorists should be conscious of the prevalence of this critical feature. If theoretical models assume uncertainty, however, and assume that agents have epistemic and ontological beliefs consistent with this state of affairs, the proper way to approach the course of economic phenomena should be very different from those that guide current modeling practice. Particularly, instead of mechanisms or economic regularities that keep running independently of agents' expectations, the decisive role of lobbyists within open-ended processes based on expectations should be incorporated into the analysis.

Such alternative approach to economics could be based on the following set of assumptions which focuses on the lobbyist role of agents and the special kind of practical knowledge and skills they need. Choosing this approach means setting aside the pretense of scientific status desired by Lucas, which is obtainable at the price of assuming STF. I suggest that the following assumptions could be the philosophical core of a new conceptual framework for economics:

1) There are economic processes based on expectations and characterized by radical uncertainty. Agents involved in such processes act in two different ways (as decision-makers or as lobbyists).

2) Ex-ante knowledge of invariant sequences of events is generally not possible (because there are few if any sequences of this kind); more importantly, such knowledge is unnecessary as support and justification for the implementation of economic policies.

3) The role of theoretical practice is to identify the many feasible "branches" of a "tree of plausible outcomes" as well as the restrictions that each sequence of events faces.

4) It is not known (and it is not possible to know) ex-ante what "branches" of the tree (what sequences of feasible alternative events) will prevail. Science cannot help us with this.

5) Other types of knowledge (common and practical knowledge as well as practical skills) are crucial for shaping those processes. It is a sort of know-how knowledge, closer to management and administration than to scientistic economics.

6) Although – as was shown in point (3) – theoretical practice has an important role to play in shaping processes, what is crucial in this endeavor is another practice, which we denote as lobbying (interventional) practice (LP). As mentioned above, LP is performed by a wide range of economic players (mostly different kind of interest

155

groups who are able to operate on the relevant context and agents' expectations).

Clarifying theoretical practice

A theoretical practice compatible with all these assumptions which incorporates uncertainty, new key players – like lobbyists – and new forms of rationality, knowledge and skills will be a huge contribution for achieving a better understanding of economic processes. It may be useful to state a few remarks to show in what sense the set of assumptions to which an economist is committed could be of relevance for his theoretical practice. One can choose to model imaginary non-uncertain worlds inhabited by ex-ante rational agents, or to analyze open ended, intervenible processes. Each approach is OK in the sense that they serve different purposes. However, if the target is real economic processes it is not easy (and maybe not possible) to build models that include uncertainty and many rival lobbyists. The essence of a model is that many things are omitted. At least this happens with those factors that are hard (or impossible) to represent within the model. All the issues connected with uncertainty may fall into this category. But, uncertainty and conflict should be incorporated to the analysis by other means. One direct way to do that is to give up making models and just talk about economics (like untrained entrepreneurs and journalists do). But if someone cannot do without models, uncertainty and conflict may be introduced into the analysis from outside of the model: via its philosophical interpretation. This is a Khunean idea: if you "see" the world through the lenses of your mental framework (paradigm), why not extend this idea and assert that looking at models and theories analysts "see" them (their content, potential and significance) trough the lenses of their ontological and philosophical framework?[7]

Consider again the so-called macroeconomic "transmission mechanisms" described in Snowdon and Vane, 1997 (see Chapter Four). What an economist sees when looking at them depends a great measure on his philosophical perspective. Anyone can register the sequence of factors portrayed by those sequences, but the significance that they have in relation

---

[7] As Edward Fullbrook makes me note, long before Kuhn, Einstein and other physicists made a good deal of this idea.

to real economic events changes according to what presuppositions one is committed to. Whether those sequences are considered as representing mechanisms that operate "behind" human actions and intentions or open-ended processes depends on philosophical commitments. Which outlook prevails will have important methodological consequences:

> 1) Those scholars who have their minds molded by the set of conventional assumptions will be committed to a mechanistic perspective, which imposes the task of choosing the "true" mechanism between the diverse sequences that are offered by different models. They will judge economic sequences to be incompatible with one another, in the same way in which, from the traditional methodological perspective rival theories cannot be all true. This way, there is no room for pluralism: the different sequences cannot be all acceptable, even if all were feasible.

> 2) Besides, if it is considered that economic theory, qua science, identifies underlying transmission mechanisms that command the processes, the political management of the economy becomes irrelevant. A commitment to standard philosophical assumptions leaves out the importance of investigating the conditions that must be met for the occurrence of what is modeled as a typical regular sequence.

> 3) Conceiving the so called transmission mechanisms as sequences of unavoidable fulfillment entails the existence of some law of expectations' formation, in order to do which it is necessary to eliminate the dissolving influence of *subjectivism* (i.e., freedom to interpret the meanings of the several informational inputs coming from the context and for guessing (imagining) future scenarios).

On the contrary, those analysts that keep in their mind the six core ontological and epistemological assumptions will see the so called "transmission mechanisms" illustrated in Chapter 4 from a different perspective.

(1) Each of them will be seen as a diagram of a truncated open process. What is depicted is just one of the many branches of the tree of feasible sequences of events. Each of them is merely a man-made sequence, which could be avoided if appropriate regulations and practical measures designed to hinder collectively undesirable behaviors are taken into account. There is no natural (inevitable) connection between self-centered agents, increments in the money supply and some definite change in output and employment. The final outcome has to be constructed. It will be the result of a political struggle that any one of the interested actors can win or lose. Although not all the feasible sequences can be realized simultaneously, any of them could be enforced. Their "rivalry" is of a very different nature from the rivalry which according to traditional methodology prevails among theories.

Mechanisms are sequences of events organized in a stable way which once triggered lead to results known beforehand. I reject the alleged *naturalness* of social sequences modeled within theoretical models. These sequences do not reflect social laws (like physical laws), or mechanisms in the usual sense of the term used in current mechanistic literature. They are just representations of truncated processes, which are open-ended in reality. Theoretical mechanisms are obtained within models assuming as "natural" and given (i.e., unchangeable as a matter of principle) institutional features that are actually historically determined and perfectly modifiable. Mechanisms are made out of processes enforcing the presence (often tacit) of regulations and institutions that eliminate otherwise alternative options.

Here is an extreme example. Full respect for private property means *absence of regulations that restrict the use of owned resources*. Obviously, if someone is self-centered, has access to a clearly optimal choice and there are no restrictions for taking it, he will certainly choose that option (whether or not it is collectively beneficial). You can then build a model that shows that, given certain changes in the situation agents will inevitably choose *this* option. A "transmission mechanism" emerges, which, in the manner of Mises, is presented as inevitable. No mention is made that one of the premises of the alleged inevitability is that full freedom is given to the agent to do as he pleases with his property.

158

If given an extreme situation (like a flood or an earthquake) nothing prevents me from increasing the price of an essential commodity that I have for sale, being self-centered I will substantially raise the price. Here is a "mechanism" (increasing demand leads to higher price), asserted by the standard economic knowledge, which works in the case of natural disasters. However, if regulations against such behavior were enforced, the predicted increase would be prevented.[8]

Someone may find it foolhardy to suggest that the principle of individual freedom for disposing of their own resources could be removed in particular circumstances. However, modern societies are characterized by the ubiquitous presence of restrictions upon individual behavior. Many sets of laws and regulations within a society have this limitative purpose. More importantly, the presence as well as the absence of restrictions on private property is strictly a social issue (i.e., the product of social conventions adopted on the basis of the existing balance of forces at the time regulations and norms are sanctioned). My main claim here is that conventional economic mechanisms are obtained assuming explicitly or tacitly crucial de-regulations (especially on big firms and mega-firms' activities) as part and parcel of the sequences of events that generate regular economic phenomena. This happens both on models and on real economies.

As suggested in Marqués (2014), the above considerations may be useful to address phenomena such as bubbles and the volatile nature of the current financial system. The absence of measures that regulate the market structure, especially the network of business connections, as well as the concentration of resources and the use that can legitimately be made of owned goods and capital, leaves the door open to economic behavior with negative impact on growth and employment. To the extent that, as some authors argue, there can be a distinction between productive and speculative activities, what is required is the creation of institutional instruments to expand and facilitate the first type of activities and temper or

---

[8] It is interesting that the city of New York has legislation that prevents this type of self-centered behavior, regulating the prices of a set of highly needed goods with the arrival of winter.

prevent those of the second type (Reinert, 2013). This seems to require an enforcement of public law over private law.

(2) The theoretical practice under conditions of uncertainty and conflict of interests (conditions where the six core assumptions described above are valid) cannot do much more than to imagine feasible sequences. It is foolish to ask more than this from a theory. In this sense it helps to be aware of the exceptionality of the conditions in which MD or PL obtain their results.

Theoretical practice offers important contributions by building credible models and identifying feasible sequences of economic events. However, the proposed framework for approaching economics shows that a good part of the success must be attributed to the incorporation of practical and common sense knowledge (the so called folk psychology), which largely preexisted the attempt to convert economic theory into science. This helps to appraise theoretical contributions on a more moderate stance. More to the point, the six core assumptions proposed above will help to reveal the central role of another type of practice, which consists in continued management to obtain targeted results in an uncertain world.

Regarding processes as the object of inquiry our distinction between theoretical and managerial knowledge is relevant. I have pointed out the difference between knowing the set of feasible sequences (which are provided by theory) and knowing how to enforce one of the sequences of the set (a task accomplished by interventions which use practical knowledge and extra theoretical skills). Looking into more familiar scenarios, it is the difference between having a good plan (*ex-ante* knowledge) and having the skills to make your plan work in practice. For this purpose the distinction seems to us useful and sound.

(3) I make a clear difference between a mechanism and a process. In the case of a mechanism its parts as well as the relations among them are stable and all of its components are shielded from external influences once started (see Glennan, 1996; 2002). Economic processes do not match this description. On the one hand, the agent´s expectations are not stable, in the sense that they are not always the same given identical changes in relevant economic factors. An increment in the supply of money may or may not be accompanied by a decrease in the interest rate, because agents' reactions to a stimulus are determined by their expectations about the future values of some relevant economic factors, values that nobody can know "scientifically" or beforehand. On the other hand, the shielding condition usually required for mechanisms is not present in the case of economic processes, which are subject to different sorts of external interventions on the part of several economic actors (some of which are made based on expectations). In our view these considerations show that no law of expectation formation exists, and in the case of economic processes it is unsound to model expectations as a part of a mechanism.

But of course one *may* model individual reactions to information. In fact, Hedström and Swedberg (1998) describe different mechanisms that typically include agent's participation. But in so doing some kind of "mechanical" (lawful) account of expectation formation has to be included. This can be done in two main ways: in an arbitrary form and using scientific resources taken from cognitive psychology. Think for instance of the "threshold mechanisms of collective behavior" (the BFM of Granovetter analysed in Chapter Four) or the "dying seminar" (Schelling, 1978), another threshold mechanism. These are cases of artificial mechanisms of decision making. In these cases the reaction to a signal of the environment (that may include the behavior of another people) is usually well defined and in some way fixed – individuals are "programmed" to react in a pre-established way. Theoretical models usually fix expectations because they seek stable sequences and well known outcomes. This lawful account of expectation formation is needed as long as theory searches for regularities. But it is baseless and artificial. A central feature of economic processes is that individual expectations are nor fixed in advance and may be influenced from outside. In most real world economic situations, when uncertainty of the Keynesian sort prevails, individual behaviour is usually volatile and subject to external influences.

On the other hand, those who dream with a vision of expectation formation subject to laws could argue that it is possible to use some kind of theoretical (scientific) knowledge to influence people's expectations. In fact, behavioral analysis may be used to influence people's decisions (i.e., framing them). There is a growing literature showing how to help people to decide among different saving or retirement plans (for instance, Benartzy and Thaler, 2007). About these issues, see Marqués and Weisman, 2011 and Ivarola and Marqués, 2012. So, it is true that in some cases theoretical knowledge may be used (and in fact it is used) to change people's minds in a desired way. Encouraged by these results someone may think that a lawful (scientific) manipulation of expectations and decisions is at hand! I disagree. The kind of theoretical knowledge provided by Prospect Theory, which gives room to the so called libertarian paternalism, is of limited application to economic processes. It works for influencing people's decisions in so far as a (unique) frame may be imposed upon them. In the simplified situation in which the only external interventionist actor is the state, Prospect Theory's tools may be useful. However, it is hard for us to see how this device could be extensively used in situations where different economic actors compete with each other to impose upon economic agents different and conflicting frames. And this is precisely the case that seems relevant in most real world situations that can be modelled as economic processes. Just as in the case of Lego!

It short, our six core assumptions to approach economics become important because they remind us that in reference to these processes the role of theory is to identify the different paths the process may plausibly take. What theory may usefully contribute in these cases is not to find out stable and recurrent mechanisms but branches of a "tree of plausible outcomes".

Going beyond ex-ante rationality

Let's consider EUT once again. Savage's paradigm of decision making under uncertainty incorporates the main features of this type of rationality. It is assumed that the subject does not know what state of the world is actually in place, but he knows all the possible states and what the results of the various actions that may be undertaken would be if the world were in any of these states. Suppose, for simplicity's sake, there are only two states, S1 and S2, and three actions a1 to a3.

S	A	C
	a1	c1
S1	a2	c2
	a3	c3
	a1	c4
S2	a2	c5
	a3	c6

The subject does not know whether the world is at S1 or S2 states, but he knows that if it is S1 and he performs action a1, the result will be c1, while if the world is at S2 he will get c4. The exercise is repeated for the other alternatives. This model of decision making is based on three basic assumptions:

1) Ignorance of the prevailing state of the world;
2) Impotence to alter that state;
3) Knowledge of the laws of nature (i.e., the connections between actions and outcomes given that the state of the world is known).

Point (1) makes it explicit what the individual is uncertain about. He is not uncertain about all the possible states (that are known). What he does not know is which of them is actually in place. From (1) and (3) it follows that he does not know which outcome he will get when performing an action. This model aims to clarify how and in what sense it might be said that an action undertaken before knowing what the prevailing state of the world is can be considered rational. I call it *an ex-ante model of deliberative rationality*. To behave rationally all that is required is that subjects be consistent with their (subjective) beliefs about the states of the world and their expectations about the results they can get by acting in a certain way. In other words, to be rational is to select the prospect (lottery) that gives him higher expected utility. Perhaps, in the end, the subject discovers that the world was not as he thought and that, therefore, the resulting consequences were not what he had imagined, but this does not detract at all from the rationality of his initial decision.

Self-validating rationality

Rationality is a key issue in economics. If ex-ante rationality is difficult to accommodate within a conceptual frame that incorporates uncertainty, may it be considered in another way? How can rationality be introduced within the framework of ontological and epistemological assumptions involved in the open-ended vision of economic processes?

If we give up the assumption (2) that agents have no power over the states of the world, and consider that there is a time interval between the action taken and the outcome, other options become available for them. An individual (or a firm) can know what the impact of *other* actions on the world will be, undertaken after what we call here the "decision" in the strict sense has been adopted. Let's suppose a lapse of time divided into two periods, t0 – t1 and t1 – t2. In t0 a subject makes the decision a1, assuming the prevailing state of the world along t0 – t2 will be S1 (the one in which c1 is expected). But then, he does not stay idle, but undertakes some additional actions b1...... bn, designed to produce (or help to create) the needed state S1. These actions, additional to (and successive to) the initial decision, are aimed at the transformation of reality in a precise way in order to get de desired result. We may call them *self-validating actions*.

A good example of validating action is propaganda, which tries to install at the top of the agents' preferences a product whose production has already been decided (or has already been finished). Let's suppose that a bad decision has been made. For instance, to produce a doll that nobody wants (something that is seen after the production process has come to an end). One solution is to change the preferences of the agents for this product. Changing preferences is an important way to change the states of the world. Remember that this was not a possibility within Savage's paradigm.

Propaganda is just an instance of a much wider repertoire of validating strategies. If a company decides to manufacture a car able to reach high speeds, it can try to ensure the existence of norms that will add value to the differential feature of its product. For instance, once its decision has been taken the company may decide to become engaged in aggressive lobbying in order to influence the sanction of new traffic rules that will be in force when the product reaches the market. The creation of new institutions is something alike to creating a complementary good for the one that is being sold.

Perfect competition models, which assume that agents lack market power, are in harmony with the *deliberative* and *ex-ante* concept of rationality. The individual or the firm, making some calculations, make a decision at an initial time t0 and then cross their arms and wait to see what fate has in store for them when the time lapse ends. In a real, not perfectly competitive market, however, there is scope for considering a different notion of rationality. Mega-companies undertake actions to reduce the competitiveness of potential rivals. They can implement practical actions and strategies aimed at creating favorable conditions for obtaining the desired results. An agent is rational not merely because he is consistent or because he is capable of performing a maximizing calculation once his interests or priorities have been defined, but because he *knows how to meet his expectations*. And he *successfully meets them*. Agents' rationality is not now of the deliberative and ex-ante type, but rather of the *practical* and *ex-post* type. Rationality cannot consist of a mere deliberative process that ends when you have chosen the best option beforehand. Not under uncertainty. There are no good (or best) options that can be recognized ex-ante. *Good choices must be constructed*. The rational enterprise strives to transform reality in a way that validates its previous decisions. The rationality of the decision originally adopted as such is revealed only at the end of the process. The paradigm of business rationality is a self-fulfilled prophecy (perhaps wishful thinking made actual by self-effort).

3. Philosophers

A theory of economic action should consider the distinctive features of economic processes under uncertainty and explain the pervasive role of lobbyists along these processes. Are mainstream philosophers of economics not interested in recovering *this* practice? The fact that they do not even try to do it is an indication that they are stuck in a philosophical conceptual framework, conditioned by the untenable assumptions of STF. Most of the current philosophy of economics is actually a philosophy of economic representations. It does not deal with economic processes but with their usual oversimplified representations (conventional economic models) which, as we have seen, leaves out of consideration the most crucial features of these processes.

Arguably conventional economic theory and mainstream philosophy of economics share their object of analysis: the world of models, but approach it with different interests, which ultimately are complementary. Theorists have constructed imaginary worlds with the purpose of examining their properties. Philosophers seek ways to provide epistemic legitimacy to this practice. They seek to develop arguments to show in what sense such models would be able to contribute to the discovery of causal connections, in what sense they could explain and predict, and how the knowledge obtained there could be profitably used in concrete applications to market economies. Naturally, it is an arduous task, which contradicts the wisdom of those who pioneered in pondering economic theory and warned that no applications could be expected from such intellectual exercises.

If an alternative theoretical practice in economics which deals with relevant problems of real economic processes is feasible, the same may be expected from the Philosophy of Economics. A relevant philosophy of economics can be developed along two interrelated lines. First it may approach features of real economies, like uncertainty, lobbying practice and the kinds of expertise and skills involved in the shaping of economic processes. Second, even if as it is usual in the philosophy of science the target must be disciplinary representations, an alternative philosophy of economic representations is possible. Specifically, one that critically examines the usual ontological and epistemological assumptions of mainstream modeling practice, and develops the basics of alternative assumptions that are consistent with the presence of uncertainty and the recognition of its existence from agents and actors. This book is an attempt to call attention to the convenience of proceeding along both these lines.

Final words to this chapter

An outline for the construction of a theory of economic behavior under uncertainty that incorporates the practice of agents as lobbyists, and examines the special way in which they might behave rationally has been proposed. It has been argued that conventional economic theory does not deal with uncertain scenarios but takes as its subject of analysis invariant regularities governing imaginary worlds. Economic theory as well as the conventional philosophy of economics, which provides its epistemic support and legitimization, deals with (fictional) representations and not with real economic processes.

Assume agents think they inhabit a world where radical novelties sometimes arise, substantially altering the prevailing state of things. Then it is reasonable to think that they also have to believe that the wider the temporary breach between the time in which decisions are taken and a later time when the results of those decisions are experienced, the less the relative importance of the present state of things to influence the state of things that will prevail at the end of the period. In such a world, the final state of things will be mainly conditioned by those states of the world that are closer to it.

Consequently, agents will think that the clues the actual state of things offers to guess the future states grows weaker the longer the considered period. This means that their ontological beliefs set strong conditions on their expectations. In these circumstances agents cannot use induction. They cannot because they think there is no relevant connection between the past and the future (at most they can think that the influence of the past on future events can be recognized only a posteriori).

Nobody can believe that the world is an open-ended process in the indicated sense and, simultaneously, that practicing induction is effective. Not without incurring in inconsistency. This provides grounds for maintaining that the first Keynesian technique cannot serve as a guide in uncertain contexts. Of course, the second one which asserts that "the existing state of opinion ... is based on a correct summing up of future prospects" is not sustainable either since it cannot be persuasive for those who think that the world is an open-ended process like the one described in Chapter Five.

But there are also no reasons to imitate other people's behavior. Assuming the world is complex, the available information is believed to be sufficient to find out the future states of things. If a limitation exists, in this case it is just of a gnoseological type. An individual could conjecture without being inconsistent that provided an agent does not suffer from that limitation he could know better than him what will happen at the end of the period. In an open ended world, however, the available information (even if it were caught in its totality) is not relevant for deciding what will happen at the end of the period.

Given uncertainty it does not matter that other subjects can have more detailed information about the present state. To imitate other people cannot be a rational strategy, not even in the weaker (coherentist and subjectivist) sense alluded to: agents cannot think that practicing imitation is an adequate answer without being incoherent with the rest of their beliefs.

The above considerations help explain why no significant concrete results ever come from the application of conventional economic models. In particular, it helps to understand why a successful applied economic science has not been established so far. It also explains the limitations of mainstream philosophy of economics to justify the epistemic relevance of conventional economic models. Our analysis has also positive suggestions. It shows that both a theoretical economic practice as well as a philosophical reflection upon it, different than the usual ones, are imaginable and points out some issues and assumptions that should be incorporated into the analysis. Our approach encourages philosophers to pay more attention to theoretical treatments of intervenible open-ended processes based on expectations as well as to agents' lobbyist practice and the kind of abilities needed to successfully influence the processes in order to obtain the desired results. These brief notes, I hope, offer an outline of a new Non-mainstream Philosophy of Economics.

.

Conclusions and further issues

Further issues – towards a general frame for approaching economic processes

This book offers a philosophical framework to promote a debate about the role of economic theory and the philosophy of economics. There is a Bookish Economics and a Mainstream Philosophy of Economics (MPE) that is also bookish because it is mainly a reflection on economic representations. But MPE is bookish in a deeper sense, because its targets are models enrolled in the tradition of bookish economics. This book is not against these two practices. Anyone is free to approach the issues they wishe. The book rather argues that another way of performing economics and philosophy of economics is available, and that it is relevant, useful and interesting. The book is an invitation and an encouragement to take this alternative avenue. It starts by making a key distinction between the domain of the economic processes and phenomena, and that of its representations. The priority of the ontological realm is assumed. If the purpose of theoretical analysis is to make a contribution to find out how modern market economies work, it must comply with the restrictions that the nature of the phenomena imposes on them. The economic phenomena result from open ended, intervenible and conflicting processes in which uncertainty prevails. Real world oriented economics has to take care of them. Nevertheless, a good amount of theoretical practice in economics treats the sequences of economic events as if they were determined by laws or mechanisms. Such practice proceeds by building models that we have characterized as "intellectual exercises". Nothing wrong may be found in such an approach, but its practical usefulness for understanding economic phenomena is unclear to say the least. There is another way of doing economics, more promising, which represents processes as feasible sequences of events. We invite practicing economists to reorient their priorities and favor this kind of analysis.

Mainstream Philosophy of Economics focuses on mainstream representations. Practicing philosophers are also invited to refocus their analysis, placing economic processes at the center of the scene. This shift could help them to visualize new problems, re-signify some key economic concepts which have actuality and clear meaning in other contexts, reconsider some crucial philosophical and epistemological issues and review the sort of theoretical practice that is relevant beyond bookish economic problems. In this book I provided an outline of this task for some selected notions like rationality, testing and learning. But much more reflection is needed about these and other topics (like the relation between science and economics and the role of practical knowledge in designing and applying economic policies) whose treatment is scant or still lacking. Its full development will allow us to clarify and to articulate a general frame for analyzing the kind of theoretical practice needed for approaching economic processes, something that diverse authors reclaim (Fullbrook, 2013; 2014). Philosophy of economics can play an important role on these matters as long as it reorients its priorities. The central points of my perspective have been already exposed in the previous pages. What follows is a summary and clarification of some thorny points that deserve to be rethought and debated.

Rationality

Davidson (2003; 2012) has drawn attention to an instrument that can be considered as an enlargement of the set of techniques that form Keynes' Practical Theory about the Future (PTF): contracts. A contract establishes a certain regularity that provides predictability about side issues concerning decision-making, such as the terms and forms of payment. Thanks to contracts many important details concerning transactions are known (there is no uncertainty about this matter), which induces agents to apply PTF without further reserve.

It should be noted, however, that both strategies (PTF and contracts) seem to be better suited for a *complex* context than for an uncertain one. PTF is inconsistent with the ontological and epistemic beliefs we attribute to agents. The first two techniques directly deny uncertainty. The third presents a somewhat different difficulty. Assuming that agents believe that the world is complex, they can consistently imitate other agents because they may believe that others have information they lack. Agents may believe this because they also believe that the information is available (they have not collected it but others may have). But if agents believe the world is uncertain, they are also committed to believe that others cannot possibly currently have the relevant information that is needed to know what decision will get the best results in the future.

Thus, contracts only contribute to "reduce" (not to eliminate) uncertainty (which strictly speaking is not removable). Because, first, the (future) values of most economic variables are not set by contract. And secondly, what ensures that contracts will be honored? Why would I be right or have a "calculable risk" for these future events? It seems that regarding contracts there emerges a second-order type of uncertainty. Of course it might be eliminated in the usual way: strengthening the PTF using the additional assumption that the conditions guaranteeing the performance of contracts today will survive in the future. But how could this belief be consistent with the belief that genuine uncertainty prevails and that future events are largely determined by events that are going to occur in the future? Think of the 2007-8's crisis. What happens with contracts when the payment chain breaks down? Crises are not exceptional, they are recurrent. And when they break out many previous contracts and agreements are violated.

Both, Keynes' PTF and Davidson's theory of the role of contracts outlined a purely passive way to deal with uncertainty. In Davidson's view contracts enter the picture as a preexisting factor in decision-making, helping to make it possible (providing more confidence in the expected result). Here I suggest a strategy to deal with uncertainty that goes the other way around. Agents who are aware that their decisions (and their results) face genuine uncertainty try to influence the course of events to reach their preferred result. When they have the power they become lobbyists, and get involved in shaping the economic process because they are aware that their further actions, those which occur *after* the decision has been taken, are the ones that will be most decisive for the final results. If there is any rationality in economic action under conditions of radical uncertainty it should be found in the agents' involvement in shaping economic processes.

In short, both approaches (PTF and contracts) are inconsistent with the assumption that at heart agents know that the value of future economic variables is presently unknowable. Ultimately, we are all Socratic in the sense that we know we do not know that. However, as long as they can, agents behave in a way that reveals their true beliefs and somehow restores consistency. When they are strong enough to affect the market they do not restrict themselves to making decisions and then sit down to await the outcome of their original actions. Rather they become actively involved in enforcing the outcome that is most convenient to them. I designate this role as *lobbying*. Agents, in addition to being decision-makers, can also be lobbyists. Assuming an active role is their way of restoring the apparent inconsistency aforementioned: agents take decisions assuming PTF and negotiating contracts, but after that they strive to influence the course of economic phenomena in order to guarantee that their original decision will finally be successful.

Note that if agents did not believe that economic issues develop in a context of radical uncertainty, they would not intervene continuously once their decisions are taken (they would not need to do that, because the result of their current decisions would be recognizable ex-ante). This is the difference between the model world and the real world. Model-world agents have (by hypothesis) all the knowledge they need to "go fishing" after their decisions has been taken. The real world is another matter. In fact, agents get involved along the processes all the time to enforce the success of their previous decisions. A vision able to give meaning to this practice is needed. That is, what is required is a theory of economic action that takes into account agents' *lobbying* role. Lobbying should be included in the agenda of theoretical economics.

Theoretical practice

There are different types of theoretical practice. In the first chapters we examined one that is oriented to the resolution of theoretical problems with maximum deductive rigor. We described it as an intellectual exercise and its usefulness to approach the relevant economic problems that arise in contemporary market economies is, to say the least, uncertain. A good number of practicing economists are busy doing these exercises, and Mainstream Philosophy of Economics strives to devise arguments intended to show their epistemic relevance. We have maintained that MPE's arguments fail and that it mistakes the very purpose of theoretical models: the solution of theoretical problems themselves, rather than finding solutions for the urgent economic problems of our world.

Nevertheless, another kind of theoretical practice is available, which was referred to in Chapter Four: the so-called mechanisms of economic transmission at macro level. Although some models of this type imagine arbitrary sequences to the only effect of reaching wished results in a rigorous way, others represent feasible (or credible) sequences of economic events. I insist on the concepts of "feasibility" and "credibility". Feasible sequences *can* happen (they are attainable in our world), although it all depends on the interventions of many different lobbyists along the process. Correctly interpreted – as open ended sequences, not as mechanisms – feasible models could be useful. Consequently, when I speak of an alternative theoretical practice I am not demanding the invention of a new way of doing economic theory (a demand that would be rather foggy). Part of the required theory is already available (I mean, the *feasible* one): it offers sequences of stages which in principle could be reached and provides points of intervention for governmental administration and the practice of private interest lobbying.

Even if a lobbyist had in mind a particular feasible sequence when pushing for results, he may be unable to attain them simply because he does not manage to gather enough strength to impose the set of institutions and measures that his project needs or because he fails to generate the expectations that his project requires. Therefore the sequence that ultimately prevails does not express some sort of standard order. Rather it has been socially constituted, and it might not have happened at all. The temptation to naturalize the prevailing social relations is huge and history is full of examples of this class. Presumed natural laws, like the incapacity of women to assume government responsibilities, have demonstrated again and again that they were just social constructions.

The main purpose of focusing on the sort of economic processes that are analyzed in this book is to show that they can be successfully managed. Particularly, I am thinking in processes in which a heterodox policy based on fuelling aggregate demand is being implemented in order to improve employment. This is why I illustrated my analysis with (a standard schema of) the so called Keynes Effect (I do not know if my two partners in my co-authored paper of 2013 agree with this view). In the case of Argentina the conventional economic view asserts that all the implemented policies designed to increase the income of the lower-wage people will be a failure. Conventional economists say so because they assume some kind of law or mechanism well known in Economics determines that fuelling the aggregate demand will result in inflation (not in more income and employment). Supposedly they know this result *ex–ante* and by *scientific* means. Other heterodox economists, on the contrary, think that the way to reach an increase in employment starts with an increase in aggregate demand. Supposedly they have discovered an alternative mechanism opposed to the conventional one! I think that no automatic mechanism able to take us (necessarily) to a success or a failure is available. Political decisions and practical measures will be crucial in the resulting events. This book is partially inspired in this controversy: we think that in the case of economic processes the final outcome is open (and there is some room for a sound administration on the part of the government).

Further Issues: pluralism, individualism and limits to interventionism

My objections to conventional modeling strategy could be extended to other forms (not only mainstream) of doing economic theory. The practice of adding suppositions of tractability for the single purpose of obtaining wished results in a rigorous way can also be used in a heterodox theoretical frame. A diversity of models (mainstream and non-mainstream) that are just intellectual exercises are readily at hand. Heterodox modeling is not by itself a guarantee of greater realism and greater applicability. More reflection is needed about the nature and the limits of the kind of pluralism demanded. Of course, pluralism is a good thing! But it may not be enough. What is required is a plurality of views that devise feasible (credible) sequences and share the basic view that economic processes are open ended, intervenible, pervaded by antithetical interests and uncertainty.

The point of an individualistic perspective also requires more reflection. Individualism has several aspects. First, it is important to distinguish the issue of methodological individualism from the role that individuals' decisions play in economic and social processes. The mediation of agents' aims and expectations is a key notion for maintaining that there are no regular mechanisms operating out there. Agents are the ones who drive economic processes through different stages of a feasible sequence and create the occasion for influencing them. Their presence allows considerations concerning subjectivism and uncertainty that would be pointless if decision makers and lobbyists were not taken into account. For that reason I distrust those who take natural sciences as a benchmark for economics, and attribute causal power to aggregate concepts as if individuals were avoidable. Particularly I feel disappointed when too much time and effort is spent in imagining situations where it would be possible to describe sequences of events overlooking individual intentions. It is wrong to think that to get rid of *methodological* individualism (a task that I fully endorse) it is necessary to leave aside individuals' expectations and goals.

Second. According to individualism doctrine individuals deserve to be free and their rights should be protected. This view presupposes homogeneity at the social level: all individuals are on equal footing regarding their influence and strength. This could have worked a couple of centuries ago, when theories as perfect competition had some ground in real market economies, but not today. Besides, assuming no collusion, the possibility that some individuals could limit the freedom or jeopardize the rights of other individuals was dismissed (except in case of criminal actions for which criminal laws were the appropriate response). Spencer is representative of this view when claiming that individuals must be protected from the State. Though it is certainly true that the State may unacceptably affect the freedom and rights of individuals, different kinds of organizations and corporations could do the same. In fact nowadays these types of interventions occur all the time and they are considerably more damaging for individuals and relatively weak economic agents. This situation opens the door for a balancing intervention on the part of the State. From an individualistic point of view it is worth reconsidering the relative power of the modern State and corporations to affect individuals' lives. From an abstract level individual freedom is an undeniable absolute value. But our concern is concrete rights and freedoms, and they are not "natural" in any sense, but socially constructed. What liberties should be guaranteed and protected is a social issue. And in so doing some other rights and freedoms could/should be restricted indeed. The case of the end of slavery mentioned in Part III clearly illustrates this point.

A remark about the *limits of interventions* will be helpful. Our analysis does not suggest that any desired result can be obtained by means of a social construction or a careful manipulation of expectations. This would be a case of blatant voluntarism, something that we do not endorse. The principle of the priority of ontological considerations also applies here, meaning that the nature of the processes sets limits not only to our representations but also to our interventions. With two caveats. First I put emphasis on *restrictions*, not on laws or mechanisms. Second, policies play a twofold role: they suffer restrictions but they can also remove some of them. All we are claiming is that even provided that "good" theory has been able to identify different feasible sequences of events (those that do not face unavoidable limitations -material, institutional or human), the path that the economy ultimately takes is decided by external intervention.

Finally, from a constructivist perspective the role of a *normative* approach to economics becomes relevant. It was dismissed within the framework of the so called positive economics – considered just wishful thinking. But as long as it is accepted that the future is not drawn up nor is it cognoscible ex-ante, and that the particular feasible sequence that is finally realized depends on what agents and lobbyists imagine and attempt to gain, there is ample space for the theoretical construction of feasible sequences. Especially for those that may lead to relevant and desired results. The technology of Libertarian Paternalism shows the way in which science may be of help. But it shows also its limits. For urgent economic problems a non-scientific and rather politically oriented "technology" (management) is needed. And it may greatly benefit from normative economic analysis.

Reorienting bookish economics

Conventional theoretical practice has not considered those central features that characterize economies as uncertain systems. Rather it has proceeded in two steps: a) creating imaginary worlds governed by regularities or invariant parameters that do not have a counterpart in real economies; b) exploring the workings of these imaginary worlds. I suggest that such theoretical practice has been developed in an inward-looking way creating its own object of study and paying no attention to economic phenomena as they occur in specific concrete economies. This is not necessarily bad, though such practice may be of no practical use.

This book does not attack such modeling strategy in itself, but rather its philosophical interpretation: the idea that mainstream theoretical models reveal the existence of economic mechanisms that work in a regular way and – this is most important – that they show that it is impossible and foolish to try to lead processes along a different path than the one pointed out by the orthodox canon. According to this school certain policies that would allow to redistribute income, or to resist the speculative maneuvers of huge economic corporations or the financial system are doomed to fail. These policies, supposedly, are self-defeating. So from the early days in which the discipline struggled to reach scientific status as "proper science" all interventionist attempts to increase or direct demand were dismissed, maintaining that what was needed was to create favorable conditions for aggregate supply. One of the main purposes of this book is to argue that many sequences considered as non-viable and prohibited by "mainstream economic wisdom" can be implemented nonetheless. If the attempt to do it fails it may be due to bad management or ineptitude to gather the political forces necessary to implement the required measures; not because there is a "mechanism" or some economic laws that prevent it.

Those authorities who manage the processes need to act as much on the context (to modify the economic factors in strict sense, but also in a more ample sense, introducing legislation, creating economic and political instruments, etc.) as on the agents' expectations. They need also to give a political fight against other actors who try to lead the process in other directions. I would like to say that there are two types of economic practice:

one that is mainly bookish, and focuses on the solutions of intellectual exercises, and another oriented to address real economic processes. I want only this second way of doing economics to be called *political economy*. What is needed to solve urgent socio-economic problems is more political involvement and management. Theoretical knowledge is also important although it plays a role along with practical knowledge and common sense (not against them).

Reorienting mainstream philosophy of economics

On this basis we have suggested the necessity to reorient Mainstream Philosophy of Economics, given that it focuses on mainstream *representations* of the "mechanisms" of market economies, not on the markets themselves. It is then a philosophy of *mainstream representations*. Besides, MPE has not managed to elaborate a theory about how such economic representations are connected with their intended targets. Without it their defense of the epistemic relevance of mainstream theoretical models and its pretension that they offer reliable knowledge about our world remains ungrounded.

On the other hand, MPE assumes mainstream economic theory's ontological assumptions. From the point of view of ME there is nothing wrong in such practice: their assumptions are the ones that the strategy of modeling chooses to represent specific aspects of interest of the model world. The problem with MPE is that it takes for granted that those assumptions are also valid in real markets, a claim to which economists do not subscribe, or at least they do not do it qua economists. The claim that what has been proven within mainstream theoretical models has external validity is not strictly economic: it is a philosophical claim. And to defend it suitable arguments are needed, something that MPE does not provide. Even worse, as far as economic processes are intervenible in multiple ways by different lobbyers, and dominated by uncertainty and conflicts of interests, there are powerful reasons to think that such defense is unattainable.

There are other aspects in which MPE also fails. It has assumed (legitimized) an ex-ante vision of the rationality of economic decisions. In addition, it has adopted a *scientistic* and *non-interventionist* attitude towards economic processes. Particularly, it has assumed the view that laws, mechanisms or invariant regularities exist, which work through markets spontaneously and dominate (overcome) the agents' decisions. The thesis that ordinary individuals or men endowed with practical knowledge are not aware of the existence of inevitable and unwished consequences of the agent's present decisions is based on that assumption.

The mainstream philosophy of economics takes for granted that the main goal of social sciences (and to MPE economics is a social science) is to discover these invariants and use them to construct explanations of social and economic phenomena. Moreover, it seems to think that these results would be useful and even indispensable for designing social and economic policies in a rational way. And most important, it assumes that the results of mainstream models de-legitimize any interventionist policy that opposes such regularities. This book has examined these arguments and found that they are not conclusive.

Bibliography

Akerlof, George A., (1970), "The Market for 'Lemons': Quality Uncertainty and the Market Mechanism", The *Quarterly Journal of Economics*, Vol. 84, No. 3, (Aug., 1970), pp. 488-500.

Alchian, A., (1950), "Uncertainty, Evolution, and Economic Theory", *Journal of Political Economy*, LVIII, February – December, 1950.

Alexandrova, A, (2008), *Making Models Count*, Philosophy of Science, 75, pp. 383–404.

Alexandrova, A, y Northcott, R (2008) "Progress in Economics: Lessons from the Spectrum Auctions" in Harold Kincaid and Don Ross (Eds.) *Handbook on the Philosophical Foundations of Economics as a Science* (Oxford: Oxford University Press, 2008).

Alexandrova, A. (2006), "Connecting Economic Models to the Real World: Game Theory and the FCC Spectrum Auctions", *Philosophy of the Social Sciences* 36: 173-192.

Aydinonat, N. Emrah, (2008), *The Invisible Hand in Economics: How Economists Explain Unintended Social Consequences*, Routledge.

Backhouse, Roger, Ed. (1997), *The Methodology of Economics: Nineteenth Century British Contributions*, Routledge-Thoemmes Press, London.

Bateman, B. W, (2003), "The end of Keynes and Philosophy?", in Runde and Mizuhara, eds, op. cit.

Bateman, B. W., and Davis, J.B., eds, (1991), *Keynes and Philosophy - Essays on the Origin of Keynes's Thought*, Great Britain, Edward Elgar.

Bechtel W. and Abrahamsen, A., (2005), Explanation: a mechanist alternative. *Studies in History and Philosophy of the Biological and Biomedical Sciences*, 36 (2), pp. 421-441.

Bibow, J., Lewis, P. and Runde J., (2003), "On convention: Keynes, Lewis and the French School", in Runde, J. and Mizuhara S., eds., 2003.

Birks, S. (2015). *Rethinking economics: from analogies to the real world*. Singapore: Springer.

Boland, L., (1981), "On the Futility of Criticizing the Neoclassical Maximization Hypothesis", *The American Economic Review*, Vol. 71, No. 5.

Boland, L., (2005), *Critical Economic Methodology: A Personal Odyssey*, London and New York: Routledge, p. 157.

Bunge, M., (1997), "Mechanism and explanation." *Philosophy of the Social Sciences*, 27 (4), pp. 410-465.

Bunge M., (2004), "How does it work? The search for explanatory mechanisms." *Philosophy of the Social Sciences*, 34 (2), pp. 182–210.

Bunge, M., (1982), *Economía y Filosofía*, Madrid, Tecnos.

Caldwell, Bruce (1994), "Two Proposals for the Recovery of Economic Practice" (in Roger Backhouse, ed., *New Directions in Economic Methodology*, London, Routledge).

Carabelli, A., (1988), *On Keynes's Method.* London and New York: Macmillan and St. Martin's Press.

Carabelli, A., (2003), "Keynes: economics as a branch of probable logic", in Runde, J. and Mizuhara S., eds, 2003.

Cartwright, N., (1999), "Vanity of Rigour in Economics" in *Discussion Paper Series*, Centre for the Philosophy of Natural and Social Science, LSE, 1-11.

Cartwright, N., (1995), "Ceteris Paribus Laws and Socio-Economic Machines", *Monist*, July, Vol. 78, Issue 3.

Cartwright, N., (2007a), *Causal Powers: What Are They? Why Do We Need Them? What Can and Cannot Be Done with Them?*, Centre for the Philosophy of Natural and Social Science, LSE.

Cartwright, N., (2007b), *Hunting causes and using them*, Cambridge: Cambridge University Press

Cartwright, N., (2008) "Models vs Parables", *Insights, Institute of Advanced Studies*, Volume I, Number 11.

Cartwright, N., (1995), "Ceteris Paribus Laws and Socio-Economic Machines", *Monist*, July, Vol. 78, Issue 3.

Cartwright, N., (1997), "Models: The Blueprints for Laws", *Philosophy of Science*, 64, s292-s303.

Bibliography

Cartwright, N., and Efstathiou, S., (2011), "Hunting Causes and Using Them: Is There No Bridge from Here to There?" *International Studies in the Philosophy of Science*, 25 (3), pp. 223-241.

Chick, V., (2002), "Theory, Method and Mode of thought in Keynes's General Theory". Presented at the Conference of INEM (International Network for Economic Method), University of Stirling, September 2002.

Colander, D., (2010), "The economics profession, the financial crisis, and method", *Journal of Economic Methodology*, Vol. 17, No. 4, December 2010, 419-427.

Cottrell, A., (1993), "Keynes's theory of probability and its relevance to his economics: three theses", *Economics and Philosophy*. 9: 25-51.

Craver, C., (2006), "When Mechanistic Models Explain". *Synthese*, 153 (3), pp. 355-376.

Darden, L., (2002), Strategies for Discovering Mechanisms. *Philosophy of Science*, 69 (S3), pp. S354-S365.

Davidson, P. (1998), "Volatile financial markets and the speculator", Paper presented as the Economic Issues Lecture to the Royal Economic Society Annual Conference, Warwick, England, April 1998 (on line)

Davidson, P. (2003), "The terminology of uncertainty in economics and the philosophy of an active role for government policies", in Runde, J., and Mizuhara S., eds, 2003.

Davidson, P. (2012), "Is economics a science? Should economics be rigorous?", *real-world economics review*, issue no. 59, 12 March, pp. 58-66. http://www.paecon.net/PAEReview/issue59/Davidson59.pdf

Davis, J. B., (1994), *Keynes's Philosophical Development*, Cambridge: Cambridge University Press.

Davis, J. B., (2003), "The relationship between Keynes's early and later philosophical thinking", in Runde, J. and Mizuhara S., eds, 2003.

Dow, S. (2003), "Probability, uncertainty and convention: economist's knowledge and the knowledge of economic actors", in Runde, J. and Mizuhara S., eds, 2003.

Dow, S., (2012a), "Different Approaches to the Financial Crisis", *Economic Thought*, Volume 1, Issue 1.

Dow, S., (2012b), *Foundations for New Economic Thinking, A Collections of Essays*, New York, Palgrave Macmillan.

Elster, J., (1998), A plea for mechanisms. In P. Hedström and R. Swedberg, (eds) 1998. *Social Mechanisms: An Analytical Approach to Social Theory*. Cambridge: Cambridge University Press. pp. 45-73.

Fitzgibbons, A, (2003), "Keynes's epistemology", in Runde, J. and Mizuhara S., eds, 2003.

Frigg, R. (2006), "Scientific Representation and the Semantic View of Theories" *Theoria*, 55: 49-65.

Fullbrook, E., (ed.) (2008), *Ontology and Economics – Tony Lawson and his critics*, Routledge, GB.

Fullbrook, E., (2013), "New paradigm economics", *real-world economics review*, issue no. 65, 27 September, pp. 129-131.

Fullbrook, E., (2014), "New Paradigm Economics versus Old Paradigm Economics" (Interview with Edward Fullbrook, Conducted by Paul Rosenberg), *real-world economics review*, issue no. 66, January, pp. 131-143.

Giere, R., (1979), *Understanding Scientific Reasoning*, Holt, Reinhart and Winston, New York.

Giere, R., (2004), "How Models Are Used to Represent Reality", *Philosophy of Science*, 71, pp. 742-752.

Giere, R., (2010), *Scientific perspectivism*, University of Chicago Press.

Gillies, D., (2003), "Probability and uncertainty in Keynes's *The General Theory*", in Runde, J. and Mizuhara S., eds, 2003.

Gillies, D., (2012), "Economics and Research Assessment Systems", *Economic Thought* 1.1: 23-47.

Glennan, S., (1992), *Mechanisms, Models, and Causation*. Ph.D. Dissertation. Chicago: University of Chicago.

Glennan, S., (1996), Mechanisms and the Nature of Causation. *Erkenntnis*, 44 (1), pp. 49-71.

Glennan, S., (2002), Rethinking Mechanistic Explanation. *Philosophy of Science*, 69(S3), pp. S342-S353.

Glennan, S., (2008), "Mechanisms". In S. Psillos and M. Curd, eds. *The Routledge Companion to Philosophy of Science*. Abingdon: Routledge, pp. 376-384.

Gordon, Robert J., (1978), *Macroeconomics*, Little, Brown and Company, Toronto.

Bibliography

Hands, Wade D., (2009), "The Positive-Normative Dichotomy and Economics". http://www.fea.usp.br/feaecon/media/fck/File/P7_Hands_Positive_Normative_Dichoto my.pdf

Häring, Norbert, (2013), "The veil of deception over money: how central bankers and textbooks distort the nature of banking and central banking", *real-world economics review*, issue no. 62, 25 March, pp. 2-18.

Hausman, D. M. (1992) *The Inexact and Separate Science of Economics*, Cambridge: Cambridge University Press.

Hausman, D. (ed.), (1995), *The philosophy of economics - An anthology*, Cambridge, Cambridge University Press.

Hayek, F., (1979) *The Counter-Revolution of Science – Studies on the abuse of reason*, Liberty Fund, Indianapolis; Primera Impresión: 1952.

Hayek, F., (1992) "The Fatal Conceit - The Errors of Socialism", in *The Collected Works of F. A. Hayek*, edited by W.W. Bartley, The University of Chicago Press, Vol. 1.

Hazlitt, H., ed., (1995), *The Critics of Keynesian Economics*, The Foundation for Economic Education, Inc., Irvington-on-Hudson, New York.

Hedström, P., (2005), *Dissecting the Social. On the Principles of Analytical Sociology*. Cambridge: Cambridge University Press.

Hedström, P. and Swedberg, R. eds., 1998a. *Social Mechanisms. An Analytical Approach to Social Theory*. Cambridge: Cambridge University Press.

Hedström, P. and Swedberg, R., (1998b), "Social mechanisms: an introductory essay". In P. Hedström and R. Swedberg, eds. *Social Mechanisms: An Analytical Approach to Social Theory*. Cambridge: Cambridge University Press, pp. 1–31.

Hedström, P. and Ylikoski, P., (2010), "Causal Mechanisms in the Social Sciences". *Annual Review of Sociology*, 36 (1), pp. 49–67.

Helbing, Dirk and Kirman, Alan, (2013), "Rethinking economics using complexity theory", *real-world economics review*, issue no. 64, 2 July, pp. 23-52.

Hodgson, G., (2012), "On the Limits of Rational Choice Theory", *Economic Thought*, Volume 1, Issue 1.

Holt, R. P. F. and Pressman, S., (2001), ed., *A New Guide to Post Keynesian Economics*, London, Routledge.

Hudson, Michael, (2013) "From the bubble economy to debt deflation and privatization", *real-world economics review*, issue no. 64, 2 July 2013, pp. 21-22.

Ivarola, L., Weisman, D., and Marqués, G., (2013), "Expectations-Based Processes. An interventionist account of economic practice". *Economic Thought.* Vol. 2, N° 2, 2013; pp. 30-42.

Ivarola, L., Marqués, G., (2012), "Behavioural Procedural Models – a multipurpose mechanistic account", *The Journal of Philosophical Economics*, V:2, 84-108.

Ivarola, L., Marqués, G., and Weisman, D., (2013), "Expectations-Based Processes. An interventionist account of economic practice". *Economic Thought.* Vol. 2, N° 2, pp. 30-42.

Keen, Steve, (2013) "A bubble so big we can't even see it", *real-world economics review*, issue no. 64, 2 July 2013, pp. 3-10.

Keynes, J. M., (2002), (first Ed.,1936), *The General Theory of Employment, Interest and Money.*
http://www.marxists.org/reference/subject/economics/keynes/general-theory/ch12.htm

Keynes, J. M., 1937, "The General Theory of employment", *The Quarterly Journal of Economics*, February, 1937.

Knight, F. H., 1995 (1937), "Unemployment and Mr. Keynes's Revolution in Economic Theory", in Hazlitt, ed., op. cit., pp. 67-95.

Knuuttila, T., (2004), Models, Representation and Mediation, PSA.

Koperski, Jeffrey. *Models.* (http://www.iep.utm.edu/models/)

Kuorikoski, Jaakko, Lehtinen, Aki and Marchionni, Caterina (2008), "Economic Modelling as Robustness Analysis", Mimeo, Department of Social and Moral Philosophy, University of Helsinki.

Kuorikoski, J., Lehtinen, A. and Caterina Marchionni, C., 2010, "Economic Modelling as Robustness Analysis", *British Journal of Philosophical Science* 61 (2010), 541–567.

Kuorikoski, J., and Lehtinen, A., (2009), "Incredible Worlds, Credible Results", *Erkenntnis,* vol. 70, n° 1.

Lawson, T., (1997), *Economics and Reality*, London: Routledge.

Lawson, T., (2003), *Reorienting Economics*, London: Routledge.

Lawson, T., (2008) "Reply to his critics", in Fullbrook, ed, 2008.

Leuridan, B., (2010), Can Mechanisms Really Replace Laws of Nature?, *Philosophy of Science*, 77.

Bibliography

Lipsey, Richard and Steiner, Peter, (1981), Sixth Edition, *Economics*, Harper & Row, Publishers, NY.

Lucas, Robert E., Jr. (1981a), *Studies in Business-Cycle Theory*, Cambridge, MA: The MIT Press.

Lucas, R. E., 1981b, "Tobin and Monetarism: A Review Article", *Journal of Economic Literature,* 19, 1981.

Machamer, P., Darden, L., y Craver, C., 2000. "Thinking about mechanisms". *Philosophy of Science*, 67 (1), pp. 1-25.

McCann (Jr), Ch. R., 2003, "On the nature of Keynesian probability", in Runde, J. and Mizuhara S., eds, 2003.

Meeks, G. T., (2003), "Keynes on the rationality of decision procedures under uncertainty: the investment decision", in Runde, J. and Mizuhara S., eds, 2003.

Mäki, U. (1992), "On the Method of Idealization in Economics" *Poznan Studies in the Philosophy of the Sciences and the Humanities*, 26: 319-354.

Mäki, U., (ed.), (2002), *Fact and Fiction in Economics: Models, Realism, and Social Construction.* Cambridge: Cambridge University Press

Mäki, U., (2008), "Realism from the lands of Kaleva: an interview with Uskali Mäki", in *Erasmus Journal for Philosophy and Economics*, Volume 1, Issue 1.138. http://ejpe.org/pdf/1-1-int.pdf

Mäki, U., (2009), "Realistic realism about unrealistic models", in *The Oxford handbook in the philosophy of economics*, ed. by Kincaid and Ross, Oxford University Press.
http://www.helsinki.fi/tint/maki/materials/MyPhilosophyAlabama8b.pdf

McCulloch, J. R. (1849), *Principles of Political Economy*, in Backhouse, 1997, Volume 4, (4.5) and (4.6).

Marqués, G., (2005), "Criticizing Dow and Chick's Dualism: the case of the dual 'rational – irrational' in the stock market" (*Post autistic economics review*, Issue nº 35, December 2005, article 4, pp. 32-39)
http://www.paecon.net/PAEReview/issue35/Marques35.htm

Marqués, G., (2013), "A plea for reorienting philosophical attention from models to applied economics", *real-world economics review*, issue no. 65, 27 September 2013, pp. 30-43. http://www.paecon.net/PAEReview/issue65/Marques65.pdf

Marqués, G., (2014), "Processes vs. mechanisms and two kinds of rationality", *real-world economics review*, issue no. 68, 21 August 2014, pp. 10-24.
http://www.paecon.net/PAEReview/issue68/Marques68.pdf

Marqués, G., (2015), "Six core assumptions for a new conceptual framework for economics", *real-world economics review*, issue no. 70, 20 Feb 2015, pp.17-26. http://www.paecon.net/PAEReview/issue70/Marques70.pdf

Mill, J. S., "On the Definition and method of political economy", in Daniel M. Hausman, ed., *The Philosophy of economics – An anthology*, Second Edition. Cambridge, Cambridge University Press, 1995. [1a. Ed.: 1836].

Mises, L. von (1996), [1949], *The Human Action*, L. von Mises Institute, Auburn.

Mitchell, S. D. (1997), "Pragmatic laws". *Philosophy of Science*, 64(4, supplement): S468–S479.

Mizuhara, S., (2003), "Keynesian convention: a textual note", in Runde, J. and Mizuhara S., eds, 2003.

Morgan, Mary S. (2012), *The world in the model: how economists work and think*. Cambridge University Press, 435 pp.

Morgan, M.S. and M. Morrison (1999) *Models as Mediators*, Cambridge: Cambridge University Press.

Morrison, Margaret and Morgan, Mary (1999), "Models as Mediating Instruments", in M. Morgan and M. Morrison (eds.) *Models as Mediators.* Cambridge: Cambridge University Press, 10-37.

Musgrave, Alan (1981): "'Unreal Assumptions' in Economic Theory: The F-Twist Untwisted", *Kyklos,* vol. 34, no. 3, pp. 377-387.

O'Donnell, R., M., (1989), *Keynes: Philosophy, Economics and Politics*, London: Macmillan.

O'Donnell, R., M., (1991), "Keynes's Weight of Argument and its Bearing on Rationality and Uncertainty", in Bateman and Davis, eds, (op. cit.).

Pettifor, Ann, (2013), "The next crisis", *real-world economics review*, issue no. 64, pp. 15-20,

Popper, K., (1996), *The Myth of the Framework*, Edited by M. A. Notturno. London and New York, Routledge.

Pressman, S. (2001), "The role of the state and the state budget", in Holt, R. P. F. and Pressman, S., eds.

Pullen, John, (2013), "Diagrammatic economics. A review of Blaug, M. and Lloyd, P. eds. *Famous Figures and Diagrams in Economics*, Cheltenham, U.K.: Edward Elgar, 2010, pp.xvii, 468. ISBN 978 1 84844", *real-world economics review*, issue no. 65, 27 September, pp. 20-29,

Bibliography

Reiss, J., (2007), Do We Need Mechanisms in the Social Sciences? *Philosophy of the Social Sciences*, 37 (2), pp. 163-184.

Reinert, Erik S., (2013), "Civilizing capitalism: 'good' and 'bad' greed from the enlightenment to Thorstein Veblen (1857-1929)", *real-world economics review*, issue no. 63, 25 March, pp. 57-72.

Rosenberg, Alex, (1992), *Economics: Mathematical Politics or Science of Diminishing Returns?*, Chicago, Chicago University Press.

Rosenberg, Alex, (2014), "From Rational Choice to Reflexivity: Learning from Sen, Keynes, Hayek, Soros, and most of all, from Darwin", *Economic Thought*, 3.1: 21-41.

Roth, Alvin E., "The Art of Designing Markets", *Harvard Business Review*, October, 2007, 118-126

Roth, Alvin E., (2002), "The Economist as Engineer: Game Theory, Experimental Economics and Computation as Tools of Design Economics", Fisher Schultz lecture, *Econometrica*, 70, 4, July, pp. 1341-1378.

Runde, J. and Mizuhara S., (Eds), (2003), *The Philosophy of Keynes's Economics – Probability, uncertainty and convention*, London, Routledge.

Scarre, G., (1998), "Mill on induction and scientific method", in Skorupski, J., ed, *The Cambridge Companion to Mill*, Cambridge, Cambridge University Press.

Shackle, G.L.S., (1967), *The years of high theory, invention and tradition in economic thought (1926-1939)*, Cambridge University Press.

Schelling, Thomas C., (1971), "Dynamic Models of Segregation", *Journal of Mathematical Sociology* 1: 143-186.

Schelling, Thomas C., (2006), *Micromotives and Macrobehavior*, W. W. Norton & Company (first published 1978).

Snowdon, B., and Vane, H. R., 1997, (Eds,), *Reflections on the Development of Modern Macroeconomics*, Edward Elgar, Cheltenham, UK.

Sugden, R., (2000), "Credible Worlds: the status of theoretical models in economics" *Journal of Economic Methodology* 7/1: 1-31.

Sugden, R., (2009), Credible worlds, capacities and mechanisms, Erkenntnis, 70: 3-27.

Syll, L. P., (2010), "What is (wrong with) economic theory?", *real-world economics review,* issue 54.

Teller, P., (2001), "Twilight of the Perfect Model Model", *Erkenntnis* 55: 393-415.

Torres, P., (2009), A Modified Conception of Mechanisms. *Springer*, 71 (2), pp. 233-251.

Roth, Alvin E., (2008), "What have we learned from market design?" Hahn Lecture, *Economic Journal*, 118 (March), 285-310

Viner, J., (1936), Mr. Keynes on the Causes of Unemployment. The Quarterly Journal of Economics, Vol. 51, No. 1 (Nov., 1936), pp. 147-167.

Weisberg, M., (2007), "Three Kinds of Idealization", *The Journal of Philosophy* 104, 12, 639-59.

Whewell, (1859), "Prefatory Notice", in Backhouse, R., ed., (1997), *The methodology of economics: Nineteenth Century British Contributions*, Routledge – Thoemmes Press, London, Volume 4 (4.7.).

White, William R., (2013), "Ultra easy monetary policy and the law of unintended consequences", *real-world economics review*, issue no. 63, 25 March, pp. 19-56.

Woodward, J., (2002), "What is a mechanism? A counterfactual account". *Philosophy of Science*, 69 (S3), S366–S377.